THEATRE LIBRARY ASSOCIATION

The Theatre Library Association is a non-profit organization established in 1937 to advance the interests of all those involved in collecting and preserving theatrical materials, and in utilizing those materials for purposes of scholarship. The membership is international and includes public and private institutions as well as librarians, curators, private collectors, historians, professors, theatre designers, actors, writers and all other interested persons.

The Theatre Library Association meets annually to conduct its business in the fall of each year. It presents a day of conferences and programs during the annual meeting of the American Library Association, usually in late spring or early summer.

Its publications are Broadside, *a quarterly newsletter, and* Performance Arts Resources, *an annual journal.*

It is governed by a constitution, which provides for a board of directors elected by the membership, and officers elected by the board.

THE THEATRE LIBRARY ASSOCIATION BOOK AWARDS

Two awards are presented annually for books of unusual merit and distinction in the fields served by the Association.

The George Freedley Award, *established in 1968, honors a work in the field of theatre published in the United States. Only books with subjects related to live performance will be considered. They may be biography, history or criticism.*

The Theatre Library Association Award, *established in 1973, honors a book published in the United States in the field of recorded performance, which includes motion pictures, radio and television.*

Works ineligible for both awards are textbooks; anthologies; collections of essays previously published in other sources; reprints; works on dance, ballet and opera; plays or scripts; and other works at the discretion of the jurors. Translations of significant works, other than play texts, will be considered. Entries will be judged on the basis of scholarship, readability, and general contribution of knowledge to the fields served by the Association. No galley sheets or proofs will be accepted. Books nominated for awards must be published in the calendar year prior to the presentation of the awards and must be received no later than March 15 of the year following publication.

Nominations are to be submitted in writing to the Chairman of the Book Awards Committee, in care of the Theatre Library Association, 111 Amsterdam Avenue, New York, N.Y. 10023.

The 1979 George Freedley Award was presented to David Garrick: A Critical Biography *by George Winchester Stone, Jr. and George M. Kahrl (Southern Illinois University Press). An Honorable Mention Award was presented to* George S. Kaufman: His Life, His Theatre *by Malcolm Goldstein (Oxford University Press).*

The 1979 Theatre Library Association Award was presented to Deciding What's News: A Study of CBS Evening News, NBC Nightly News, Newsweek & Time *by Herbert J. Gans (Pantheon). An Honorable Mention Award was presented to* American Film Now: The People, the Power, the Money, the Movies *by James Monaco (Oxford University Press).*

PERFORMING ARTS RESOURCES

Edited by Mary C. Henderson
with the assistance of Wendy Warnken

VOLUME SIX

Published by the Theatre Library Association

The Library of Congress cataloged this serial as follows:

Performing Arts Resources
    Vols. for 1974- issued by the Theatre Library Association
      ISSN 0360-3814
1. Performing arts — Library resources — United States —
Periodicals. I. Theatre Library Association
Z6935.P46 016.7902'08 75-646287
ISBN 0-932610-02-1

Produced by Publishing Center for Cultural Resources, NYC
Manufactured in the United States of America

TABLE OF CONTENTS

PERFORMING ARTS RESOURCES, *the annual publication of the Theatre Library Association, is designed to gather and disseminate scholarly articles dealing with (a) the location of resource materials relating to the theatre, film, television and radio and (b) a description, listing or evaluation of the contents of such collections, whether public or private.*

All manuscripts must be submitted cleanly typed, one side only, double-spaced and adhering to the style and method described in the MLA Style Sheet, Second Edition. *Since PAR will attempt to cover a wide area, articles of extraordinary length or technical prolixity will be admissible only in rare circumstances. Photographs and illustrations may be used at the discretion of the editorial board.*

Please submit manuscripts with covering letter and return postage to:

Performing Arts Resources
c/o Barbara Naomi Cohen
300 Riverside Drive #11B
New York, New York 10025

AN EDITORIAL VIEW

Shortly after I arrived at the Museum of the City of New York to join the Theatre Collection staff, I received a call from a young woman who told me that she had just taken over the job of handling and cataloging the immense aggregation of the Federal Theatre Project papers which had come to George Mason University under an agreement with the Library of Congress. Her name was Elizabeth Walsh and she wanted to visit our collection to attempt to find out how best to achieve this formidable task. I told her that my contribution would be a 'how-not-to-do-it' object lesson. Within a few weeks she arrived in New York, and I gave her a tour of the collection before we began serious talk.

From that point on, Elizabeth and I talked and wrote to each other frequently. I admired her uncommon good sense, her sure-footed approach, and her dedication to the enormous job of sorting through the exciting papers of an exciting era in theatrical history. Although the frustrations were many and profound, I knew that she wanted to do the job right from the beginning. I could sense that she derived satisfaction from what she was doing and from the realization that she could make a significant contribution to theatre research if the collection at George Mason was well organized.

Elizabeth's untimely death brought to an abrupt close the fulfillment of her aims. But all of us who remain know that her work was not in vain and that her successors were able to pick up where she left off and move toward the completion of the work she so earnestly began.

While she was alive, I caught her enthusiasm for the Federal Theatre Project documents. She invited me to George Mason University to see them for myself. So impressed was I that I asked whether she would consider preparing an extensive set of essays for a single volume to be dedicated to new theatrical collections in America. Despite her overwhelming schedule, she readily agreed and over the next months sent me groups of short essays on the work-in-progress. After her death, Laraine Correll took over Elizabeth's job and inherited the task of updating all of the articles which I had received. They are here published as an editorial collaboration of two dedicated people along with descriptive essays of other collections which have arrived on the scene during the past decade. Since the inspiration came from Elizabeth Walsh, I would like to dedicate this volume to her memory.

And with this volume, my editorship of *Performing Arts Resources* comes to an end. I have learned much from my five years and three volumes of PAR and this special knowledge has already been put to good use in other ways. I wish to thank the board of the Theatre Library Association for the confidence shown in me by allowing me a free hand to shape each publication as I saw fit. It has been my pleasure.

New York, 1980   Mary C. Henderson

FEDERAL THEATRE PROJECT RECORDS
AT GEORGE MASON UNIVERSITY

The information presented in this article was written in short sections by several knowledgeable individuals:

Carol Baxter, Library Assistant, Special Collections at George Mason University, wrote the material on music records.

Margi Berkowitz, editorial consultant and former staff member of the Research Center for the Federal Theatre Project, advised and assisted in the overall editing of the article and co-authored the material on production notebooks.

Lorraine Brown, Professor of English at George Mason University and Associate Administrator of the Institute on the Federal Theatre Project and New Deal Culture, wrote the material on radio scripts and co-authored the material on audience surveys, playreader reports, production notebooks, and oral history.

Jeanne S. Burch, formerly Coordinator of Researcher Services for the Research Center for the Federal Theatre Project, wrote the piece on photograph materials.

John Y. Cole, Jr., Executive Director, Library of Congress Center for the Book, co-authored the material concerning the Library of Congress role in the receiving and storing of the Federal Theatre Project archival records. Portions of his material appeared in an article titled, "WPA Research Materials at the Library of Congress: A Review and Progress Report," Library of Congress Information Bulletin (*November 29, 1974, pp. A243-A245*).

Laraine Correll, formerly Director of the Research Center for the Federal Theatre Project and currently Head of Special Collections at George Mason University, was general editor of the article; wrote the introduction and the material on the intellectual and physical control of the FTP records; and co-authored the pieces on administrative records, research records, and oral history.

Brenda Zanger Greene, formerly Coordinator for Public Services of the Research Center for the Federal Theatre Project, co-authored the material on design records.

Roberta Gupta, formerly a graduate assistant of the Research Center for the Federal Theatre Project, co-authored the material on play-reader reports and audience surveys.

Sharon Leuthy, formerly a graduate assistant of the Research Center for the Federal Theatre Project, co-authored the pieces on design records and promotional art.

John O'Connor, Associate Professor of English at George Mason University, and associated with the Institute on the Federal Theatre Project and New Deal Culture, wrote the material on the FTP records at the National Archives and other libraries, George Mason University acquisitions, and playscripts. He co-authored the pieces on administrative records, research records, and promotional art.

William J. Sittig, Technical Officer for the Library of Congress Collection Development Office, co-authored the material on the Library of Congress role in receiving and storing FTP records.

Elizabeth Walsh, late Director of the Research Center for the Federal Theatre Project, wrote the piece on the history of the Federal Theatre Project. This material appeared in different form in Dramatics Magazine *(March/April 1977) based on her participation in a series of lectures on the Federal Theatre sponsored in 1976 by the Department of Theatre and Drama of the University of Wisconsin at Madison.*

Karen Wickre, former Oral Historian for the Research Center for the Federal Theatre Project, co-authored the oral history material.

Introduction

Scholars and librarians have entered into a partnership at George Mason University to create significant resources for the study of the Federal Theatre Project (FTP) and New Deal culture. The resources concept transcends a physical place. In addition to collecting primary and secondary research materials, GMU has gained a reputation for being a moving force behind the interinstitutional and interdisciplinary study of the literature, theatre, music, and art of the period in American history known as the New Deal Era.

Taken together, the Federal Theatre Project and the New Deal Culture collections at GMU number about 250,000 items. The materials may be thought of in terms of four major groupings: (1) administrative records, including personnel folders, publicity clippings, meeting notes, financial data, reports, policy and procedure memorandums, mailing lists, and correspondence; (2) research records, including bibliographies and lists, card files, playreader reports, study guides, reports on sources of dramatic literature, factual research for productions, audience surveys, and the Living Newspaper clipping file; (3) production records, including billboards, posters, photographs, music, prompt scripts, film clips, programs, lighting plots, costume and set designs, production notebooks, marionettes, radio scripts, and publicity materials; and (4) nonarchival Federal Theatre Project materials, including books, magazines, articles, speeches, unpublished research, and oral history memoirs.

The larger share of these records has been placed on permanent loan by the Library of Congress on the condition that the materials be sorted, inventoried, and made accessible to scholars. This group contains duplicate material which will be returned to the Library of Congress for their Exchanges and Gifts Program. FTP records which did not come as part of the major deposit have been donated to the University by hundreds of former FTP employees whom the University has contacted. In addition to the archival records, the University has acquired related books, articles, and unpublished research dealing with the Federal Theatre Project or New Deal culture. Through an oral history program, 250 individuals have been interviewed (using both audio and videotape) to create new documentation for the period. The University has also initiated and cooperated in projects which resulted in performances and broadcasts of FTP dramatic material and in scholarly conferences, and the documentation for these projects has been deposited in the collection for public research.

Annually, hundreds of researchers visit the University for a tour or for intensive research activity. Theatre company representatives come to study the dramatic resources available for their productions; authors come for information and illustrations for books and articles; students, from high school level through post-doctoral level, conduct research for term papers, theses, and dissertations; faculty prepare curriculum materials for courses in theatre, history, economics, arts administration, English, black studies, and American studies; journalists visit for background information on articles or broadcasts; former FTP personnel visit to assist the staff in unraveling certain mysteries and to prompt faded memories of an exciting period in their lives; and sometimes people come to review memories of being in audiences for FTP shows. In the five years since the materials have been at George Mason, over 3,000 people have come into contact with the materials through research or through the many programs based on the FTP and its records. To solidify communications with those eager to learn more about FTP studies, 12 issues of a newsletter, *Federal One,* have been distributed to the mailing list of one thousand names.

The University agency responsible for this extraordinary activity, which included the unpacking, sorting, and processing of the deposited material, was the Research Center for the Federal Theatre Project. Established in 1975, the Center was initially headed by Dr. Michael Sundell in association with Dr. John O'Connor and Dr. Lorraine Brown (who had been instrumental in the placing of the FTP records at the University). Elizabeth Walsh was the curator. A major research collection grant was received from the National Endowment for the Humanities for the sorting, organizing, and inventorying of the materials and to start an oral history program. Other grants, making possible much of the progress and success of the early years, were received from the National Historical Publications and Records Commission to survey FTP materials in private hands, from the Rockefeller Foundation for an experimental video history program, and from the Meyer Foundation for assistance with exhibits and the newsletter. In 1978, Dr. Sundell left the Center in order to pursue other research projects based on America in the thirties, and Elizabeth Walsh became the Director of the Center and head of the University Library's new Special Collections department. Ms. Walsh died in January 1979 and Laraine Correll took over the joint responsibilities.

After five years of intensive work on the FTP records, the University has committed itself to an expansion of the research collections and attendant academic programs. The new focus will place the FTP records as one part of a larger research collection on New Deal culture. Administrative changes were made this year to allow the research faculty involved in this program increased university support, while placing the care, cataloguing, and public service aspect of the Research Center in the hands of the expanding Special Collections Department. The Research Center for the Federal Theatre Project has been phased out, and the Institute on the Federal Theatre Project and New Deal Culture has been established under the University's Center for Government, Society and the Arts. The faculty and staff of the former Research Center have been realigned within the new administrative structures. Dr. Sundell is welcomed back as the administrator of the Institute, with Dr. O'Connor and Dr. Brown remaining as associates. Individuals at the Institute can be reached at the Institute on the Federal Theatre Project and New Deal Culture, Fenwick Library, George Mason University, Fairfax, Virginia 22030 (703/323-2546). Laraine Correll is the head of Special Collections, and can be reached at Fenwick Library, George Mason University, Fairfax, Virginia 22030 (703/323-2251).

The Institute already has a number of exciting projects underway. Among them are the planning of a major FTP exhibit exploring post-doctorate fellowships with area cultural institutions, a series of public and scholarly programs dealing with government support of the arts, and a joint conference with the National Archives and the Library of Congress on interdisciplinary approaches to the New Deal culture records held by GMU and these institutions. Special Collections is reorganizing some of the research materials, working on preservation projects, and continuing work which will result in the publication of a register of the FTP records by the Library of Congress. Work is almost completed for a calendar of FTP productions (with holdings list and indexes) to be published by Greenwood Press. Another important project involves the coordination of the various FTP finding aids.

The research records are made available to scholars through the University Library's Special Collections Department, in Fenwick Library on the main university campus. All visitors are welcome to view exhibits, and individuals with specific research goals are encouraged to use the materials. Access to the collection is through personal visit, mail, or telephone inquiry. Appointments are encouraged to avoid delays in service when visiting in person. The hours of service are 8:30 to 5:00 weekdays and are subject to change due to staff leaves. Evening and weekend appointments may be arranged for special circumstances. The Library is open between academic terms and closed for the standard holidays plus the time between Christmas and New Years. Researchers are required to submit an interview statement on a form provided by the Department. It is recommended that this form be submitted by mail prior to a campus visit. In addition to identification information and details of the research project, the form requires a signature acknowledging fair use regulations and reading room regulations. Researchers cannot handle materials in person or receive facsimile copies of materials by mail until an approved interview form is on file. A new form is required for each new project. Staff works with new researchers at the beginning of the visit to orient them to the diverse bibliographic tools available for the research collections. The finding aids are discussed in detail in the last section of this article.

The majority of the materials in Special Collections are released for facsimile copying. Student assistants are available at hourly minimum wage to copy approved materials for researchers if the copying takes longer than one-half hour. If given specific approval, the researcher may be allowed to copy some materials personally. Checks are accepted (payable to George Mason University) and estimates are furnished for telephone and mail inquiries. Special orders are required for other types of copying such as photographic prints, negatives, slides, microfilm, audio and videotapes.

Staff search services for mail and telephone requests are provided free of charge if they can be completed within an hour. Student assistants are available at minimum wage for additional service authorized in advance by the researcher.

Interlibrary loan of selected items is permitted and researchers must request this service through their local university or public library system. Reading copies of scripts are lent to performing and broadcasting companies for selection considerations. Once a script has been selected for performance or broadcast, additional procedures will be discussed.

Requests for special services should come in writing and with as many details included as possible. Tours may be arranged for small groups. Speakers for classes or groups may also be arranged. Requests to exhibit collection materials, either originals or facsimiles, must be made in writing. Most of the materials from the Federal Theatre Project Archives requires permission and handling of the Library of

Congress, a process which takes a minimum lead time of three months. To appreciate the nature of the FTP records at George Mason University requires backtracking to a brief history of the agency which produced the records (Part I) and then following the records through a complex system of deposits and transfers through various archival institutions and private individuals (Part II).

Part III imparts more specific information on the nature and research value of the materials. The processes of bringing the materials under physical and intellectual control is discussed in Part IV.

I. The Federal Theatre Project, 1935-39

What was the Federal Theatre Project? In 1935, when the federal government decided that actors, artists, writers, and musicians had to eat too, it established, under the Works Progress Administration (WPA), the Federal Arts Projects. All of the Arts Projects were intended not only to provide employment for professional artists, writers, and performers but also to generate a renaissance of the arts directed toward the populace of the United States at large. It was this idea of a new national audience that provoked much of the excitement and controversy surrounding the Federal Arts Projects.

Hallie Flanagan, the woman chosen to head the Federal Theatre Project, described it thus:

> It was the idea that art was as much the concern of the government as agriculture, that the best art is that art which can be enjoyed by all the people, and that a truly national art for the U.S. means something which is within the geographical as well as the financial range of the average citizen.

For theatre, the plan was to create out of the economic crisis and the chaos of the times a federation of national theatres, each one indigenous to the area and people it served. With this idea in mind, plus the realization that the Federal Theatre owed its existence to economic necessity, Hallie Flanagan set out to give the public good, low-priced plays which ideally, at least, spoke to their economic and social problems.

As a result, FTP produced many plays on contemporary issues. It also produced the classics, melodramas, comedies, circus, vaudeville, and local pageants. The fare was as diverse as the audiences' tastes and the actors' abilities. In addition, FTP supported research into theatre in other countries, American theatre before FTP, and innovations in stage techniques and theatre technology.

Before examining the successes, contributions, and failures of the Federal Theatre, we need to look at the people for whom this project was established. The unemployed professionals included actors, technicians, stagehands, older performers squeezed out of the commercial market, vaudeville and circus performers clinging to skills no longer needed or wanted, and young people not yet with established reputations — people like Abe Feder, Howard Bay, Orson Welles, Joseph Cotten, and Norman Lloyd. Some of the unemployed needed to be retrained in skills rusty from lack of professional use. The young needed direction, training, exposure, and a chance to try out their ideas.

Not unexpectedly, many of the unemployed persons with the requisite ability for theatrical enterprise turned out to be persons with new ideas. That private industry and particularly Broadway found no use for their talents is one of the indictments of commercial theatre in the 1930s, where making money was the primary criterion.

These were the people hired by the Federal Theatre for $23.86 per week. And these were the people who not only offered the good, low-priced plays that Hallie Flanagan wanted, but also created seminal productions through experimentation with new forms and content — another effort in which she was interested.

Reactions varied. There were those who denied that people without money or jobs should be fed, and there were even more who denied that people without money should be entertained. Many Americans with jobs saw themselves as examples of the survival of the fittest, as living proof that hard work brings material rewards, and they wanted the unemployed to keep their place as foils to their success.

The unemployed were almost universally enthusiastic about the Federal Theatre, especially because it quickly gained an enviable reputation as the largest producer of quality plays. The uncharitable attitudes of both audiences and reviewers diminished as it became clear that the Federal Theatre welcomed thoughtful criticism and that unlike commercial producers it took an interest in its audiences.

The audiences increased by a million for every million spent and none of those millions was being spent for publicity. The Federal Theatre depended on news releases, reviews, word-of-mouth, and quality to lure the audiences to its plays. The variety of productions playing to people in schools, hospitals, churches, clubs, and parks as well as in regular theatres gives an indication of the vast numbers of people who saw Federal Theatre productions. In the summer of 1937, in New York City alone, nearly two million people attended the Caravan Theatre plays in the city parks. By 1939, Hallie Flanagan estimated that more than twenty-five million people had attended Federal Theatre plays.

The better part of the audience at any FTP production had never seen live drama before. Its educational value alone in training new audiences is one of its most valuable contributions to American theatre. Thus, the Federal Theatre did not compete with private enterprise, in spite of occasional charges to that effect, but rather broadened the base of support upon which commercial producers could mount their shows.

Another major contribution made by Federal Theatre to American drama was the Living Newspaper. Growing out of the need that Hallie Flanagan identified from the start — the need to recognize the poignant struggles of the American people to confront the economic and social problems of their society — the Living Newspaper attempted to address issues in dramatic form. This kind of dramatic journalism demonstrated the resolution, for some theatre people, of the problem of the artist's relationship to society.

Hallie Flanagan in *Arena,* her book on FTP, described her feelings about the political commitment of drama this way:

> In an age of terrific implications as to wealth and poverty, as to the function of government, as to peace and war, as to the relation of an artist to all these forces, the theatre must become conscious of the implications of the changing social order, or the changing order will ignore, and rightly, the implications of the theatre.

The Federal Theatre did not ignore the implications of the changing social order. Its form of response was the Living Newspaper:

Triple-A Plowed Under, on agriculture; *Injunction Granted,* on the history of the labor unions' struggles with the courts; *Power,* on private ownership of utilities; *One-Third of a Nation,* on the housing situation; *Spirochete,* on venereal disease.

The Living Newspaper focused not so much on current news items as on the dramatization of a problem composed of many news events and informed by extensive research. Gathering together numerous aspects of current issues required editorial writing that led to the development of a unique theatrical form. All the Living Newspapers had several things in common: great speed, compression of material, resourceful use of light and sound, a keen awareness of human values in the social order, and a shrewd use of direct exposition. Using those techniques prompted an identification between the characters in the plays and the members of the audience. An idea clearly and dramatically presented draws the audience to the realization that changes are possible.

The Federal Theatre Project also provided a new avenue of expression to large groups of people formerly excluded from participation in theatre activities. Most significant was the chance it gave to black artists to speak as writers, actors, directors, lighting experts, and costume and stage designers in the legitimate theatre. It gave them training as well as an opportunity to step out of stereotyped roles both on and off the stage — to do professional work in a professional theatre. Members of the black community capitalized on this chance and the Negro units produced some of Federal Theatre's most noteworthy productions.

The New York unit at the Lafayette Theatre put on classics (like its famous "voodoo" *Macbeth* production), musicals, modern melodrama, and such new plays by and about Negroes as *Turpentine* by J.A. 'Gus' Smith and Peter Morrell, *The Conjure Man Dies* by Rudolph Fisher, and *The Trial of Dr. Beck* by Hughes Allison. In Los Angeles, Hall Johnson's *Run Little Chillun,* directed by Clarence Muse, ran for more than a year and was seen by more than 30,000 people. Seattle's Negro unit had a big hit with its production of Theodore Browne's *The Natural Man,* a folk-opera version of the John Henry legend. The Chicago unit's "swing" *Mikado* was so successful that commercial interests competed to buy it from Federal Theatre. That group also produced Theodore Ward's *Big White Fog,* a drama that many judged to be the best social play of Negro life produced by Federal Theatre.

The establishment of ethnic groups within the Federal Theatre followed from Hallie Flanagan's hope to create a theatre which should reflect our country, its history, and its diverse regions and populations. The foreign-language groups produced plays in German, French, Spanish, Italian, and Yiddish.

Federal Theatre's goal of reflecting our country and its population led to the creation of an active and imaginative dramatic program for children. In considering children as people to be entertained, FTP made a valuable contribution in an area of theatre long neglected by commercial enterprises. The conviction that children belong in the audience, not on the stage, resulted in Federal Theatre productions that delighted adults as well as children. In every major region of the country, children were being offered plays, musicals, and marionette shows. Yasha Frank's *Pinocchio*, using vaudevillians with their perfect sense of timing and knowledge of how to milk a situation, was one of the Federal Theatre's most popular plays. It was still running when the announcement came that the Federal Theatre was to be no more, and the audience participated in a funeral for *Pinocchio*, who had just been killed by Act of Congress. *The Emperor's New Clothes*, another popular play, boasted imaginative costumes and sets as well as music by Lehman Engel. *The Revolt of the Beavers*, by Oscar Saul and Louis Lantz, stirred up a controversy that figured heavily in the 1938 hearings before the Dies Committee (the House Committee on Un-American Activities labeled *The Revolt of the Beavers* a communistic play, its authors saw it as a children's allegory only — those hearings were pivotal in bringing about the demise of the Federal Theatre Project).

At the same time, in New York, a marionette unit under the direction of Remo Bufano produced *Treasure Island, Sherlock Holmes, String Fever, Ferdinand the Bull* and numerous other shows. Across the country, marionette and children's units were operating in Boston, Cleveland, Gary, Tampa, Jacksonville, Miami, Orlando, New Orleans, Charlotte, Raleigh, Durham, Goldsboro, Manteo, Oklahoma, Dallas, Chicago, Omaha, Los Angeles, San Francisco, Denver, Seattle, Wilmington, and Newark. In California, Ralph Chessé not only produced the marionette shows *The Jewel Tree, Alice in Won-*

derland, Rip Van Winkle, and *Hansel and Gretel,* but he also traveled the state teaching the history of puppets, demonstrating how to manipulate the marionettes, and sharing his know-how about building marionette stages and even the puppets themselves. This effort to teach new skills or to upgrade skills was practiced throughout the Federal Theatre, not just in the marionette units. It was a conscious effort to continuously retrain workers and to expose them to new techniques of staging, lighting, costuming, make-up, and acting. The Federal Theatre supported experimental units in California and New York which tried new techniques in actual productions: a try-out unit which put into production new plays before recommending them to Federal Theatre units across the country; and a workshop unit designed to train costume and stage designers, actors, lighting people, and directors.

In looking at the Federal Theatre to evaluate its contribution to American theatre, one accomplishment demands special attention: the Federal Theatre gave young people a chance to experiment and kept many now-famous young professionals in the craft who might have been lost to the theatre forever. Among these can be listed Orson Welles and Abe Feder who worked, with John Houseman, at the Lafayette Theatre in Harlem. Their production of *The Tragical History of Doctor Faustus* is memorable as a successful presentation of a classical play using innovative lighting and staging. Howard Bay, then a young stage designer, designed the realistic set for *One-Third of a Nation,* among other plays. The set consisted of a three-story cutaway of a tenement built with steel scaffolding, which was set on fire at every performance. Numerous actors were discovered in Federal Theatre plays, including Joseph Cotten, John Randolph, Norman Lloyd, John Huston, and Will Geer. George Izenour began his career by lighting shows for the Federal Theatre. For the preservation and development of talent, the Federal Theatre stands as the bearer of a large and important segment of American culture.

Add the circus and vaudeville productions; the innovative dance productions of Helen Tamiris, Don Oscar Becque, Myra Kinch, Ruth Page, and Katherine Dunham; the playlists compiled and circulated across the country; and the scholarly work sponsored by the FTP's National Service Bureau (including a history of eighteenth- and nineteenth- century social drama, a history of the Chinese theatre in

America, and the "Annals of the San Francisco Stage"); and the Federal Theatre's place in theatre history becomes firmly established. Much that is hailed as original and innovative today had its groundwork laid between 1935 and 1939 in the Federal Theatre.

II. Disposition of Federal Theatre Project Records, 1939-80
In December 1940, the Washington office of the Works Progress Administration deposited at the Library of Congress some 30 file cabinets of Federal Theatre Project National Office records and 25,000 miscellaneous FTP publications for arrangement and inventorying. These were the first FTP materials to arrive at the Library. Their arrival was part of a series of deposits and transfers between 1939 and 1946 which made the Library into a major federal repository of the publications, research materials, and administrative records of Federal Project Number One. This project, known as Federal One, was the principal arts program of the WPA and consisted of five distinct projects: the Federal Art Project, the Federal Music Project, the Federal Writers' Project, the Historical Records Survey, and of course, the Federal Theatre Project. A conservative estimate is that approximately 5,000 cubic feet of arts projects materials were forwarded to the Library from WPA offices throughout the nation during those seven years.

The Library of Congress's role as a repository began shortly after the demise of Federal One in 1939, when a special Library of Congress WPA Project was established with the financial assistance of the District of Columbia WPA. This project undertook editorial and technical work and, later, the collection, preservation, and organization of WPA records.

During 1940, the state WPA projects were instructed to send their records, publications, and research materials — including works-in-progress — to the central WPA office in Washington, D.C. The response was generally good, except that relatively few state projects forwarded work in the visual arts. The WPA office transferred the bulk of the material received from the states to the Library. In most cases, ownership was also transferred, even though certain categories of documents and manuscripts remained "on deposit" for several years before the title passed to the Library. By the spring of 1941 there were over 80 full-time employees in the Library WPA Project.

Their task was made difficult by the completely disorganized condition in which most of the materials arrived.

One of the Library WPA Project's accomplishments was the complete arrangement and checklisting of the Federal Theatre Project records received from the WPA Washington office. The project was unable, however, to devote full attention to the second significant group of FTP materials received in the Library — the Vassar College Loan Collection of FTP records. This large collection consisted of administrative and production records from the New York City FTP office and included FTP's National Service Bureau playscript and music libraries. FTP National Director, Hallie Flanagan, had originally persuaded the WPA to lend this collection to Vassar College for its theatre research project but sent it to the Library in May 1941 on instructions from the Washington office. In July 1941, before the Library could turn its attention to this collection, the Library's WPA Project was terminated.

Even though the project and its staff were abolished, the Library remained actively interested in the WPA materials. Subsequently, the proper deposition of the Federal Theatre Project materials became a cooperative effort between the Library and the National Archives.

The Archives, which had supervised the processing of state and local Federal Theatre Project records in New York City, had been receiving large quantities of FTP materials also. By a series of transfers of FTP materials between the Library of Congress and the National Archives in 1943, 1944, and 1946, the Archives assembeled, for the most part, the administrative records and "official" file of product records of the FTP, and the Library maintained the second set of product records and other publications. Over 500 cubic feet of WPA administrative records, of which approximately 75 percent were from the FTP, were transferred in October 1944 from the Library to the Archives.

Transfers from the Archives to the Library included entire boxes of commercial playscripts, original musical scores, costume and scenery designs, posters and billboard signs, duplicate copies of typed and mimeographed playscripts, radio scripts, play lists and catalogues, and miscellaneous reference books and magazines. In 1947, the Library sent over 900 cubic feet of FTP materials, presumed to be duplicate items which had been transferred from the Archives, to the Veterans Administration office in New York City for distribution to VA hospitals throughout the country. The VA returned some 70 boxes containing material for which it had no use.

Although the Library did not process completely the massive numbers of WPA materials in its custody, a major inventory was compiled in 1949 by Frances T. Bourne, an archivist then on the staff of the National Archives. Miss Bourne not only thoroughly described the collection and tagged the nearly 300 containers for easier identification and access, but she also made suggestions regarding the disposition of the materials. Her recommendations to destroy more than half the collection, including the Federal Theatre Project materials, were not accepted by the Library. Instead, the Library added the published FTP volumes to the Library's classified collections, assigned many of the nonbook items to the special collections, and disposed of some of the duplicate material, primarily commercial paperbound and typewritten playscripts, through exchange and gift channels.

The remainder of the collection retained by the Library was for many years stored in the Capitol Hill buildings. In 1963, a final review was made by the Library's subject specialists. They agreed that despite its bulk and its many duplicate materials, the collection was of sufficient value to be preserved — even if the Library was forced to store it off Capitol Hill. Then, in 1964, because of the squeeze for space, the entire unprocessed WPA collection was placed in storage at Middle River, Maryland, just east of Baltimore. Subsequently, it became difficult to service the material to scholars and researchers because of the remote location and because the only guide to the storage collections was Miss Bourne's 1949 inventory.

In the early 1970s, as Depression-era culture became an increasingly popular field of study and the Library of Congress realized it could not make the Federal Theatre Project Collection easily and quickly accessible, it took measures to place its collection on deposit at George Mason University in Fairfax, Virginia. The University assumed the responsibility in August 1974 for housing, organizing, and servicing the FTP Collection in accordance with the procedures and policies of the Library of Congress.

The history of the Federal Theatre Project materials at the Library of Congress was characterized by the receipt and transfer of large groups of records; occasional projects to examine, evaluate, and sort the collection; and the integration of significant numbers of items into its general and special research collections. It is important to note that for the greater part of the period in which the FTP Collection was in the custody of the Library there was comparatively little scholarly interest in the creative products of the 1930s. The Library was not organized to serve as a major center for the study of the American theatre, and the institution was experiencing serious space problems at its Capitol Hill locations. Although the Library was never able, due to many other priorities, to house and arrange adequately all of the FTP materials in its custody, it had the foresight to realize the collection's potential as a source of scholarly interest and took measures to preserve it from destruction or unnecessary dispersal.

The majority of the FTP records at the National Archives in Washington, D.C. are administrative and research materials. Although there is some duplication, these records are generally not available elsewhere and are a valuable supplement to the production materials in the collection.

The Archives' holdings provide interesting examples of the operations and red tape that were the necessary framework for Federal Theatre productions. They contain information as diverse as FTP Director Hallie Flanagan's National Office correspondence, regional personnel applications, publicity and press clippings, requests for tickets, and research on Indian dance drama in the Southwest.

The material is inventoried under Record Group 69 (Records of the Works Progress Administration) and is located on three floors in the Archives building. A large part of the collection — primarily but not exclusively print material — is housed on Floor Eleven-E. The Audio-Visual Division on Floor Eighteen-E houses photos, FTP radio show recordings, and some designs. On the twentieth floor in the Motion Picture Division are several short films about the Federal Theatre Project.

The papers on the eleventh floor fill more than 590 document boxes and 32 shelves. After this material was deposited at the Archives, a preliminary checklist and series of appendices were drawn up. In general, these list the contents of most of the 590 boxes and, in some cases, the contents of the individual file folders within the boxes. Copies of the appendices, as well as more detailed lists compiled by the staff at George Mason, are available at the University.

Appendixed files range from the National Office General Subject File (with a 19-page list covering 28 document boxes), and the National Office Correspondence File (which fills 43 boxes), the National Service Bureau's (NSB) General Subject File (12 boxes) and NSB's Research Department Correspondence File. Also listed are playscripts, production bulletins, and NSB research studies.

These appendices are invaluable to researchers because the actual materials, maintained in the original working order, are filed so erratically. Some are filed alphabetically by name of person, some by state, some chronologically, and some by a combination of the above. In the National Office General Subject File, for example, the titles run the gamut from "Acknowledgements" and "Box Office Statements" through complaints, play titles, job analysis sheets and procedures for time-keeping, to "Unique Letters" and "Blanche Yurka's Tour." The general files of the National Service Bureau (which did research and provided plays for FTP units) include subjects as diverse as agents' letters and audience surveys, Dramatist Guild contests, expired contracts, reports from staff, material about the translation department, and of course, references to individual play titles. The NSB's Research Department files are divided into Eastern and Western regions and cover such subjects as the minstrel show, ballads of the Revolutionary period, and histories of actual theatre buildings and of national and ethnic theatre traditions (Chinese theatre in San Francisco, for example).

Like the general files, the correspondence files cover a wide variety of categories. Some contain mostly paperwork with regional offices, interdepartmental memos, and many general reports. The letters of top Federal Theatre officials, including Hallie Flanagan, William Farnsworth, John McGee, Howard Miller, Robert Schnitzer and others, fill 14 boxes. Much of this correspondence is the kind of routine letters and memos expected in a government relief operation, but mixed in with the usual requisitions and inventories are valuable nuggets of information and insight.

In addition to the general and correspondence files, there are 16 boxes of publicity material, 4 of testimonial letters, and 15 of press clippings reviewing Federal Theatre plays across the country. Also included with this material is other promotional literature for the project, as well as 28 set and costume designs (Item 85 on the Archives checklist) mostly from West Coast shows.

In the Audio-Visual Division on Floor Eighteen-E are sound recordings (and a few tapes) of some FTP radio shows, representing about two dozen series from 'Accident Prevention' through 'Jules Verne' to 'Women in the Making of America.' Also in this section are roughly 14,000 Archives photos of Federal Theatre productions and approximately 35 designs. The photographs are organized by state, then unit. Spot checks indicate considerable duplication with the photographs at George Mason. The designs are from West Coast productions and are, of course, unique. Six costume designs by Nelson Baumé for *Run Little Chillun* are the most striking of this group.

In the Motion Picture Division on the twentieth floor are eight short films depicting different phases and areas of Federal Theatre Project operations, with the concentration on California units. One of the films is a survey of the Federal Theatre from the *March of Time* series. It includes film clips of the stage productions of *It Can't Happen Here* and Orson Welles' "voodoo" *Macbeth*. Another film covers the Federal Theatre's contribution to the San Francisco Exposition where a special outdoor theatre was built on Treasure Island and six shows were performed daily. The University has videotape copies of the Archives films.

While the Archives and Library of Congress collection on deposit at George Mason University are central sources for Federal Theatre Project materials, some university and public libraries in areas where FTP operated also have holdings. The Theatre Collection of the New York Public Library at Lincoln Center has the largest holding outside Washington, D.C. Some of the materials in these collections are unique, but often they are duplicates of the Federal Theatre Project's mimeographed publications, sent to major libraries by the FTP National Service Bureau in 1937 and 1938. Some collections are supplemented by the personal papers of individuals who were in the Federal Theatre Project.

The following list includes all other library collections known to have FTP materials. The staff would welcome inventories from any other libraries holding Federal Theatre Project records.

Detroit Public Library: press clippings, 2 playbills, lists of productions.

Harvard University: 36 Play Bureau publications (scripts and playlists).

Indiana University: Orson Welles collection and the Mercury Theatre Archives.

Museum of the City of New York: research records.

New York Public Library: FTP publications, press clippings, playbills, theatre and radio scripts.

Princeton University: *Federal Theatre* magazine, regional FTP publications, playbills, press clippings.

San Francisco Public Library: Western Region theatre research, programs, reviews.

Seattle Public Library: playbills.

University of California-Los Angeles: radioscripts, scripts, playlists, John Houseman Collection.

University of Florida: programs, scripts, *Federal Theatre* magazine.

University of Iowa: E. C. Mabie and Don Farran Collections.

University of Kansas: clippings, playscripts, playlists, FTP research publications.

University of Pittsburgh: Play Bureau publications (scripts and playlists), programs.

University of Southern California: plays from the Los Angeles Regional Service Bureau.

University of Washington: FTP History of Washington theatres, photos, letters.

University of Wisconsin: Marc Blitzstein and Emmet Lavery Collections.

Yale University: programs, FTP research and regional publications, *Federal Theatre* magazine.

Because of the sudden closing of the Federal Theatre Project and the political atmosphere that pervaded the congressional hearings and conferences on the FTP, many Project workers kept Federal Theatre records rather than send them to New York and Washington, D.C., where they feared the records might be destroyed or censored. The University has been steadily acquiring these items as individuals recognize that now they will be properly appreciated. Some of the materials, like mimeographed playlists or copies of *Federal Theatre* magazine, are duplicate items; but others, like sheet music, set models, designs, audience surveys, and production notebooks, are rare and extremely valuable. These records fill significant gaps in the Federal Theatre story, especially when they came from areas outside of New York City.

Some notable arts projects publications that have been donated are the Nebraska folklore pamphlets, published in 18 mimeographed volumes and covering topics from cowboy songs to children's games; the history-of-the-drama study guides which were used in Florida schools where performances toured; and various FTP National Service Bureau magazines including *The Prompter, Call Board, Federal Theatre in the South* and *Continental Theatre*. Other official Federal Theatre records include production notebooks for the Living Newspapers *One-Third of a Nation* and *Medicine Show;* heavily annotated stage manager's scripts for *Sing for Your Supper, O Say Can You Sing* and *Swing It;* photographs of the Texas Centennial production of *Follow the Parade* and the Seattle Negro unit's campy *The Taming of the Shrew;* and many playbills from productions across the country.

Along with these official Federal Theatre records, many individuals have donated personal scrapbooks, clippings, books, memos, and letters from the period. Of these private materials, the scrapbooks are often the most exciting and informative. Besides playbills and play reviews, they frequently include private items that offer glimpses of behind-the-scenes life in the Federal Theatre Project. Personal letters and memos are rich in detail. The photographs are often candid and taken backstage by amateurs. (Three pictures of a *Horse Eats Hat* rehearsal, taken by professional Rudy Burckhardt, are exceptions.) Some of the newspaper clippings are feature articles about a unit or a particular member of it. Others relate the current rumors of cutbacks, closings, and scandals. By studying the scrapbooks a researcher can begin to understand the pride, anxiety, and uncertainty of individual workers in the Federal Theatre.

The scrapbooks and the many newspaper clippings help illuminate in particular the Boston, Florida, Seattle, and Southern California units, as well as the New York City Living Newspaper unit. Nine scrapbooks from four individuals in Florida (two from former FTP Florida State Director Dorothea Lynch) offer an enormous amount of detailed information about the Federal Theatre Project in a state that was a tense mixture of Northern and Southern traditions. Ten scrapbooks of Howard Miller, who was deputy national director and West Coast regional supervisor, provide an extraordinarily full history of the Western Region, especially the Southern California units. One scrapbook is devoted entirely to the *It Can't Happen Here* productions; another is filled with magazine articles about the Federal Theatre. The Miller scrapbooks are the cornerstone of the Howard Miller collection which also includes books, playbills, photographs, personal correspondence, press releases, and budget information.

Similar large, individual collections have been donated by Kate Drain Lawson, Arnold Sundgaard, and the estate of Adams Rice. Lawson, a designer and research administrator for the Federal Theatre, gave administrative correspondence (including press releases for 18 New York City shows), fact sheets, schedules and statistics for Federal Theatre productions, and personal memos and correspondence. Oliva Hudson, daughter of Adams Rice, a technical director for the New York City Popular Price unit, donated clippings and documentation, most notably for *It Can't Happen Here* and *Murder in the Cathedral.* The Arnold Sundgaard collection includes not only the author's Federal Theatre works (*Spirochete* and *Everywhere I Roam*), but also much of his later work, such as the Broadway-produced *Of Love Remembered* and the Mormon pageant *Brigham.* Sam Leve, one of the principal designers for the Federal Theatre, has donated sketches for sets and working set models for *Tobias and the Angel* and *The Cherokee Night,* which were produced at the Provincetown Playhouse in New York.

A similar nonprofit group of artifacts comes from one of the marionette units, which were an important part of the Federal Theatre in many cities. Many finely-crafted puppets and marionettes are still in the hands of their creators; occasionally some have been offered for sale, but the University has lacked funds to purchase them. Recently, however, Molka Reich, a puppeteer with the Miami unit, donated the handsome marionettes and props for the "rude mechanicals" scene in *A Midsummer Night's Dream.*

III. Research Value of the Records
Considering the tempestuous history of the Federal Theatre Project, the complex dispersal of its records and the significant efforts of insti-

tutions to preserve and make the records accessible, the researcher will find a closer look at the surviving documents useful. The section below describes and provides details on such categories in the collection at George Mason as: administrative records, research records, production records, and nonarchival Federal Theatre Project materials.

Since only a fraction of the total collection can be noted here, it should serve to whet the appetite of researchers interested in American and foreign dramatic resources, government support of the arts, national theatres, folklore, regional theatre, ethnic theatre in America, political and social issues in the arts, arts administration, black theatre and drama, technical theatre, children's theatre, marionettes, radio, management of information resources, theatre architecture, careers of any of the 12,000 individuals on the FTP payroll, women in the arts and government, social and educational organizations of the 1930s, labor, communism, vaudeville, circus, the Civilian Conservation Corps (CCC), or artistic and literary rights.

Administrative Records. The administrative records are the smallest group of FTP archival materials within the University collection, but they provide valuable background and insight into the Federal Theatre Project's organization and decision-making process. (It should be remembered that the bulk of the administrative materials is at the National Archives.) The records vary from personnel folders, which give biographical information, to authorization slips and interim reports. Numerous reorganization plans, operations manuals, and policy guidelines reflect the continual state of change in which the FTP functioned. The travel reimbursement and transfer forms suggest some of the governmental red tape in which the project was frequently entangled. On the other hand, files like the Play Policy Board minutes and other conference reports reveal the vitality and imagination that helped define the Federal Theatre.

The correspondence in the collection is mostly interdepartmental memoranda from the playwriting section. These discuss such matters as author's rights, operating procedures, funding difficulties, and possible productions. There is an interesting series of letters between Ben Russak, head of playwriting, and John Gassner. There are also many letters and memos concerning the playwriting contest jointly sponsored by the project and the Dramatists Guild.

Inventory lists of equipment, books, and office supplies can be found in the files. Library catalogues of major theatre libraries were solicited or compiled. There are a large number of mailing lists for such diverse groups as drama critics, women's organizations, labor groups, and agricultural colleges. Between the administrative and research records, over 50 card file sets have survived. The card files come in three sizes (3 x 5, and 4 x 6 and 5 x 8) and many colors and in some cases with colored metal signals for further coding. A few of the sets appear to be carbon duplicates. The file divisions, coupled with the color codes and the signals, can be quite complex. Some information is filed on cards which appear to be master files for various published bibliographies and lists. Seventeen double catalogue drawers list plays alphabetically by title with information on length, locale, period, acts, costumes, and age and sex of characters. One card file lists Hallie Flanagan's speeches as well as articles by and about her. Other card files list songs used in FTP productions (four sets: one filed by title, one by publisher, one by type of song and one by state in which the production was given). The Talent Bureau casting cards are wonderful sources of information on actors of the period and their resumes. Supply requisitions were also maintained on cards.

It is possible to trace interpretations and effects of governmental bureaucracy on creative and artistic enterprises through the administrative records. One of the most revealing (and heftiest) documents is the brief prepared by the staff in the agency's defense against the charges made by Martin Dies's Committee on Un-American Activities. Although it was never allowed to be entered into the official record of the committee hearings, it is a remarkable compilation of testimony to the achievements of the Federal Theatre Project and the processes through which these accomplishments were made.

Until the archival records were made available to researchers, much of our information on the Federal Theatre came from contemporary feature news and magazine articles. The National Service Bureau's Department of Information placed most of these articles, which appeared in such magazines as *Fortune, Life, Scholastic, Commentary, Magazine of Art, Theatre Arts,* and *The Saturday Evening Post.* The major New York newspapers also frequently printed articles on aspects of the Federal Theatre. Many of these were placed in clipping files along with lists of all articles, features, and editorials about the FTP and its productions. Some articles can also be found in scrapbooks in the collection.

Research Records. The Federal Theatre Project research records encompass diverse materials from a variety of sources. Their core consists of the records of the National Service Bureau and the New York Departments of Research and Information. The NSB — which due to frequent reorganizations was also known as the Bureau of Research and Publication and the National Play Bureau — was meant to be a national clearinghouse of information on the local FTP units. The NSB searched for and evaluated plays, collected information about FTP productions, collected press clippings and photographs, researched and distributed technical theatre information, and coordinated the schedules and activities of the local units. It also supported a massive research program in foreign drama, early American drama, American theatres and theatrical history, audience surveys, bibliographies, and factual evidence for topical and historical plays.

Much of the NSB materials were shaped into lists or bibliographies. Although hundreds of lists were compiled or collected, only about 25 playlists were published. Topics range from "American Folk Plays" and "Rural Plays," through "Anti-war Plays" and "Labor Plays," to "Catholic Plays" and "Jewish Plays." These lists give a brief synopsis and basic production information (such as number of set changes, number of roles and intended audience). Plays actually produced by FTP were listed by region with information on the length of run, attendance figures, and amount of money collected. A few lists were made on early theatre productions in a particular city. For example, Catherine Henry, a New York City researcher, analyzed 15,000 playbills in the New York Public Library's Theatre Collection and compiled a list of productions and their literary sources. Bibliographies were collected on make-up, costumes, lighting, theatre techniques, puppetry, and motion pictures. Other bibliographies were composed to support research for factual plays. The wide-ranging topics included housing, medicine, American Indians, "famous lives" books for children, and Iowa, Oklahoma, and Appalachian folklore. Many lists were prepared on books or legends suitable for dramatizations.

Other kinds of research could not be packaged into lists, so synopses were written. Material was collected for, and reports written on, foreign theatres, including the theatres of China, Germany, Ireland, Italy, Japan, Mexico, Poland, and Russia. Most of the reports had a historical perspective and were supplemented by surveys of contemporary drama and modern techniques in acting, design, and staging. Early American theatre and ethnic theatre in America were also researched. There are book-length manuscripts on "Chinese Theatre in America," "Jewish Theatre in America," and "American Social Drama." Histories were written on the theatre in Seattle and San Francisco and on such individual theatres as the Goodman in Chicago, the Ritz and Adelphi in New York, and the Copley in Boston. Additional histories cover such types of theatre as caravan theatre, circus, American opera, pageants and cycles, children's theatre, and CCC camp entertainment. Five manuscripts relate the growth and vitality of vaudeville and include detailed descriptions of some vaudeville sketches. Three booklets describe 56 minstrel sketches, 59 comic monologues, and 57 variety skits. Much of this research material was intended to revitalize old forms and popular genres as well as to inform FTP units across the nation of the great possibilities offered by foreign theatre and theatrical innovations.

Research was also done on subjects that might be turned into good drama. Briefs on the lives of famous people, such as American presidents and well-known historical figures, were written, with extensive bibliographies attached. Important women and black Americans were also occasionally the subjects of biographies. For instance, Abram Hill researched and wrote a scenario on the life of Booker T. Washington. Novels and topical books were analyzed for possible dramatization — Jack London's *Martin Eden,* for example. Some topics that were considered potential dramatic material and researched in great detail were the lumber and cotton industries, the history of labor and work relief, Boulder Dam, the American city, and housing. These topics were usually explored from many angles — historical, social, political, and economic. In some instances, a scenario was included along with the prose synopsis of the research. Norman Rosten's work on immigration and the Pittsburgh steel industry culminated in *The Iron Land* and John Silvera's research on slavery and the history of the Negro was the basis for *Liberty Deferred.* Behind much of this research and the plays that resulted — in particular the Living Newspaper — is a massive clipping file known as the Living Newspaper Morgue. Newspaper clippings — enough to fill 56 drawers — were cut and filed according to subject by FTP clerks for use in playwriting research. The clippings come primarily from the New York City newspapers, and subjects range from the general, such as "Business Trends and Elections," to the specific, such as "Fingerprinting" and "Japanese Beetles." Another part of the morgue is a file cabinet of clippings of photographs. Again the subjects vary widely. The news photos reflect current events as diverse as the Joseph Kennedy children boarding a ship to England, the 1939 World's Fair, and the floor plan of the *Hindenburg.* Several files document not only FTP events but also other WPA arts projects.

In addition to providing subject matter for potential plays, research efforts had to yield an effective system for reading and reporting on actual playscripts — whether they were written by FTP personnel or by outside playwrights. Although playreaders were employed by FTP in Los Angeles and Chicago, the Playreading Bureau in New York produced most of the approximately 50,000 playreaders' reports now in the collection, which illustrate how this need was met.

The Playreading Bureau originally was part of the Bureau of Research and Publication under Rosamond Gilder; it was made a separate entity in May 1936 under Francis Bosworth, then was centralized under the Play Policy Board early in 1937. In July of that year, the bureau found a permanent home in the National Service Bureau (NSB) — a merger of the Play Bureau and the Play Policy Board which resulted from budget cuts. Emmet Lavery then became director of the Play Department, with Converse Tyler heading the playreading staff, Ben Russak supervising the playwriting and Benson Inge coordinating the translation of plays.

The bureau operated for four years and employed approximately 130 readers. A large proportion of them were new, unproduced writers for whom playreading was a means of earning a living while they worked on their own scripts. When one of these writers completed a script, he was free to sell it commercially or he could submit it to the Federal Theatre, which would work out a royalty agreement with the writer. Thus, theoretically at least, FTP would have a source of new plays and writers could hold their own copyrights.

Each reader was required to read one script per day and write a one-page report. They were supposed to report daily or, in some cases, weekly. Theoretically, there were to be three readers to each script. If all three rejected the script unreservedly, it was returned to the author or shelved until a later date. If a script was recommended by even one of the three readers, it was to receive further readings.

The following two readings — from a total of six — of Arthur Miller's *They Too Arise* show the kind of diversity that could occur.

Anglo-Jewish Theatre
Leo Schmeltsman
January 18, 1937
Title: "They Too Arise"
Author: Arthur A. Miller
Publisher: Unpublished
Type: Drama
Theme: A strike
Acts: 3 (6 Scenes)
Characters: 25 (22m, 3f)
Important Characters: 3 (3m)
Characters: Abe Simon, a clothing manufacturer
        Ben
        Arnold, his sons
Settings: 3. A parlor; an office; a meeting-room
Time: The present   *Place:* New York City

Synopsis: Abe Simon, a clothing manufacturer, loses his business because he refrains from hiring strike breakers during a clothing workers' strike. Roth, a rich manufacturer, visits him and, informing him that he intends to retire and leave his fortune to his only daughter Helen, expresses the desire of having Benny, Abe's son, for his son-in-law. To save his parents from poverty, Benny, who does not love the girl, is willing to marry her. But when Abe discovers that Roth has employed strike breakers and deprived him of his customers, he breaks off the negotiations and orders the rich and greedy man to leave the house.

Comment: A plotless, incoherent, undramatic and uninteresting piece. It has a few lines of good humor and smooth but juvenile and pointless dialogue.   Leo Schmeltsman

Title: "They Too Arise"
Author: Arthur A. Miller
Address: 411 North State St.,
          Ann Arbor, Michigan
Reader: Lipschutz
Type: Social Drama
Acts: 3   *Sets:* 3
Characters: 16   *Extras:* 10
Men: 13   *Women:* 3
Date Read: Feb. 10, 1937

Summary: Abe Simon, a clothing merchant, stricken with bad business and a strike on his hands, takes out his aggravations on his family, particularly his old father-in-law. He is trying to interest his son Ben, already in his business, to marry one Helen Roth, uninteresting daughter of a rival. When Arnold, his younger son comes home from college, Abe gets him to come down to the shop to help out, but Ben is determined to prevent Arnold from making deliveries thru the strikers' picket-lines, of which Arnold, already a radical, is ignorant. At the shop Ben almost goes mad trying to get shipments thru somehow to the customers before their merchandise is recalled by the manufacturers. In desperation, Ben and Abe go to a meeting of their association. The bigger men are determined to hire strikebreakers to make shipments, etc., and are about to railroad a vote to that effect. Abe and Ben try to defeat the vote for terrorism, but lose. Later, they lose their orders, and the shipments are taken away from them. At home, Ben is about to succomb [sic] to his father's request that he marry Helen Roth, when questioning her father, they learn that it was Mr. Roth who used unscrupulous business methods to take away from them the order that was to keep them in business. The grandfather now dead, Abe is penitant, [sic] for his blind unkindness. He is determined to change things while working as a laborer with his sons.

Comment: This is an exceedingly promising play, just fitted for the Anglo-Jewish Theatre since it deals with the problems of a sigificant [sic] strata of American Jews. There are weaknesses in dramatic structure, and the dialogue is often heavy. The play is really dramatic for all these weaknesses, and the characters are convincing, the most convincing I have found in any script coming into the Bureau for some time.

A sincere effort. It must be encouraged and accepted with recommendations for revisions.

When conflicting reports surfaced or a script contained "controversial material" a special reader was called in or the script was read by Converse Tyler or Ben Russak who made the final decisions. *They Too Arise* ultimately was produced for one night in Detroit. Another play, Annie Nathan Meyer's *Black Souls,* was not produced, apparently rejected because of its "controversial material." *Black Souls* deals with a love affair between a black teacher-poet and a white senator's daughter. The poet is lynched when the affair is discovered and the girl allows everyone to believe she was raped. The point of the drama was to expose and deplore "the prejudice that holds a Negro responsible in every association with whites." The first reader found the script "stirring and true but too inflammatory for production." The second reader found it "interesting but far-fetched and with no real characters." An unsigned report found the play to have "tremendous force and sympathy in richly dramatic terms." The reader called in to summarize the other reports considered it "a very strong and potent dose for the majority of readers."

In addition to reading the scripts provided, readers were encouraged to find their own. Many of these naturally were library copies of classics or already popular modern plays which could be adapted to the needs of the Federal Theatre. Thus, William Shakespeare, Ben Jonson, Maurice Maeterlinck, Karel Capek, and Maxwell Anderson are names that turn up under "author" on the readers' reports.

Readers also solicited scripts from friends and acquaintances and the bureau received scripts from writers who, for a variety of reasons (their political views, for example, or the experimental nature of their writing), apparently felt that their work would stand a better chance with Federal Theatre than with commercial theatre.

Play themes vary from light comedy and romance to contemporary social and political issues, so that a study of the readers' synopses and comments provides comparisons between the established popular theatre of the thirties and the movement taking place in that era toward greater realism and representation of all social and ethnic groups.

The quality and quantity of the readers' individual work varied considerably. There may even have been a hierarchy among the playreaders. Some readers, in fact, made summaries of and drew conclusions from the reports of others. Although this may have been done on a rotating basis, the same names recur, which makes it appear to have been a special assignment. Special readers were also assigned to read black and other ethnic plays. Some readers obviously were more zealous than others. Some used three or four sheets for a single assignment, ignoring printed directions to produce one page. Others offered only the most cursory and unhelpful comments, such as "Scrap this!" "Didn't like it!" "Such tripe!" But most were conscientious and many reflected a thorough knowledge of good theatre, and eagerness to try new things, and a flair for recognizing talent and potential talent in the disfigured and much-revised scripts of inexperienced writers. However, the ghost of a well-made play still hovered in the air, which occasionally impeded the appreciation of more experimental work.

Among the readers were Rose F. Carlyn, who wrote plays for the children's theatre (some of which are in the collection) ; John Silvera, co-author of *Liberty Deferred,* a Living Newspaper on the experiences of blacks in America ; Hopwood Award winners Norman Rosten and Arthur Miller; and Converse Tyler, William Beyer, Brian J. Byrne, H. L. Fishel, Ruth Morris, Herb Meadow, and John Rimassa, who were all on the list of "playwrights of the ninety best new plays" compiled by Francis Bosworth and Converse Tyler to call attention to new talent (mostly within the ranks of FTP) .

As one reads through the reports, one begins to recognize readers' names and personalities; to predict what kind of script a particular reader will approve or reject; to recognize personal ideals, biases, gripes, and also — since the readers were not inhibited in their comments — what they thought of the Federal Theatre, their immediate employers, and each other. Thus, besides being entertaining reading, the reports provide a more vivid impression of the life within the Fededral Theatre than any more formal account.

Reader Katherine Roberts' report on *Bird Wing* is one example of the kind of revelations that go beyond strictly dramatic criticism. *Bird Wing* was a play in which the central character, a successful career woman, gives up her career to marry a man who tyrannizes her. Katherine Roberts was so appalled by the values in this play that she forgot the critique and delivered a lecture on how a woman *should* react in such a situation. She noted that the woman character in *Bird Wing* should answer the man's contempt "with a swift kick" and walk out forever. (Although, according to Katherine Roberts at least, women fared badly in *Bird Wing*, women who worked as readers do not seem to have suffered discrimination. There were fewer women readers than men, but the names of those who were employed appear on reports as frequently as those of their male counterparts.)

Because the readers were reviewing scripts written by women, by blacks, and by young political reformers, the playreaders' reports provide researchers with a source of contemporary comment on almost any aspect of the 1930s, besides documenting and helping to explain the theatrical preferences and experiments of that era.

Because of the large number of playreaders' reports in the collection (about 50,000), their catalogue is still in progress. The reports are filed alphabetically by play title with all reports on a title in the same folder. Often attached to the reports is other relevant material such as correspondence, special readers' reports, or memoranda on technical difficulties or difficulties with subject matter.

Another segment of FTP research records in the collection is the audience survey. Federal Theatre's Audience Research Department was established in August 1936, when research workers were sent into New York theatres to interview members of the audiences. The questions they had been instructed to ask were then incorporated into a questionnaire card to be distributed to future audiences.

In October of the same year, the first official survey of audience reactions was launched when questionnaires were sent to all units throughout the country which were producing *It Can't Happen Here* (see sample at end of article). From that date until budget cuts in 1937 eliminated the surveys, questionnaires were routinely handed out at Federal Theatre productions in major cities. Regional directors were also requested to prepare surveys for their areas, compile results into an audience survey report, and return copies of the reports to the Audience Research Department in New York.

An obvious benefit of the surveys was, of course, the growing list of people desiring continuation of FTP. Equally vital was the use of the survey as a "constructive critic" to help producers correct and modify production features which audiences found unpalatable. For example, on the basis of audience criticism, the background music for *It Can't Happen Here* was toned down. Technical features of *Noah* and *Sweet Land* were corrected on the basis of questionnaires. Even the ending of *Sweet Land* was changed. The Living Newspaper also incorporated audience suggestions and used them in preparing subsequent productions.

The original plan of the Audience Research Department was to begin the surveys with a play's opening and run them for a week. The results would then be compiled and given to the managing producer in report form. Both regional and national FTP administrative personnel would also receive copies.) Two weeks later, another survey would be made to see if the suggestions had been acted upon and to determine the audience reaction to the play at that time.

Audience reaction to Federal Theatre plays continued to be favorable in the months following inauguration of the surveys at the production of *It Can't Happen Here*. An ongoing file of plays most frequently requested was compiled as a guide to the types of plays the Federal Theatre should produce in the future.

Survey data made it clear that the Federal Theatre had a growing audience, many of whom were attending the legitimate theatre for the first time. The figures provided a fairly conclusive answer to those who claimed that the Federal Theatre constituted a threat to the commercial theatre. In fact, a sizeable portion of Federal Theatre's audiences had their only contact with the theatre through its plays. Not surprisingly, the usual reason given for infrequent attendance at the theatre was "the expense."

Audience Survey Reports, except in fragmentary form, were not among the product materials in the collection at George Mason University. But from the fragments, and from a perusal of the reports in the National Archives FTP collection, it became clear that at least sample copies of the surveys should be available for scholarly use at the University. At present in the collection, there are copies of 50 Audience Survey Reports covering about 15 major productions during the years 1936 and 1937.

Although the surveys varies from region to region, reports are about six pages in length. The format is as follows: Page 1 gives the title of the production covered, dates on which questionnaires were issued, and the region or city in which the survey was taken. Page 2 lists the occupations of audience members and the number of persons questioned in each occupational group. Page 3 lists general questions and records responses with the number of times each response was made. For example, in answer to the question, "How many Federal Theatre plays have you seen?" the audience response at *Captain Brassbound's Conversion* in the Hollywood Playhouse, Los Angeles, October 21, 1937, was as follows:

25 attended for the first time

93 attended from 2 to 5 plays previously

75 attended from 6 to 12 plays previously

47 attended all or nearly all

6 had no reply

This format was used for all the general questions which were aimed at discovering if and why Federal Theatre appealed as an alternative to the commercial theatre and the movies.

Pages 3, 4 and 5 record the comments of the audience on particular features of a production, and on the production as a whole. Comments are usually brief but cover direction, performance, music, content, technical features, costumes, set, make-up, house management, and attitude toward admission prices. The final question asked is whether audiences favor a permanent Federal Theatre. Responses to this question were recorded numerically. The last page provides a summary of findings for the production.

The reports in the collection are from the New York City, California, Texas, and Colorado units. They include *The Tragical History of Doctor Faustus, Einmal Mensch, Hansel and Gretel, It Can't Happen Here, Macbeth, Bassa Moona, Candide, How Long Brethren? Noah,* and *The Show-Off.*

The Audience Survey Reports provide accurate and useful information about audience reaction to Federal Theatre production and, in the summaries, information about Federal Theatre's policies regarding its audiences in the earliest days of FTP. However, conclusions about audience building and support that occurred after 1937 when the Survey Department was abolished necessarily remain subjective and speculative. An example of an audience survey questionnaire follows.

The Audience Is The Best Critic
AUDIENCE SURVEY QUESTIONNAIRE
for *It Can't Happen Here*

1. Is this the first Federal Theatre play you have seen?
2. Which do you prefer, plays or movies?
3. Do you go to the theatre often? If not why not?
4. Would you like a *permanent* Federal Theatre? Why?
5. Would you like a Federal Theatre in the community where you live?
6. Do you prefer plays which deal with current issues such as *It Can't Happen Here?*
7. Have you any critical comments, or any suggestions which would make this play more satisfactory to you?

Name:
Address:
Occupation:

(Wherever possible announcement of Federal Theatre plays will be sent to you)
PLEASE HAND THIS QUESTIONNAIRE TO A THEATRE ATTENDANT

F.T. Unit	Play Bureau
Place of Perf.	303 W. 42 St.NYC

Production Records. The Federal Theatre Project production records at the University are the heart of the archival collection and, as far as we are aware, the most complete source of FTP production records. Recent staff research reveals that in the five years the FTP was in operation, more than 2,400 different productions were selected or written, researched, cast, designed, rehearsed, and in most cases played, to audiences of millions of Americans across the country.

The University doesn't have complete record sets on each production, of course, but there are complete or nearly complete sets of records for hundreds of productions and fragmented sets for hundreds more. Some of the more important record categories are described below; however, the types of record categories include: billboards, cast lists, correspondence, costume designs, costumes, film clips, financial records, ground plans, heralds, lighting cue sheets, lighting plots, marionettes, music, photographs, playbills, playscripts, playscript sides, posters, production notebooks, programs, property lists, publicity reports and clippings, radio scripts, research reports, reviews, scenarios, scrapbooks, set designs, set models, study guides, and technical reports.

Playscripts. The 5,000 Federal Theatre Project playscripts are the single largest category of materials in the collection at George Mason University and may be considered the frame around which the rest of the material is organized. The actual number of play titles is considerably fewer (approximately 2,500), since a large number of the plays have multiple mimeographed or carbon copies. For example, there are 31 copies of *It Can't Happen Here* (one signed by Sinclair Lewis) and more than 100 copies of a marionette script, *Don Quixote,* On the other hand many plays exist in a single, fragile typescript. In general, however, the scripts are remarkably well preserved.

The script collection includes everything from vaudeville scenarios and comedy sketches to plays by classical and established authors to new unproduced scripts by unknown authors. All together, it clearly substantiates the Federal Theatre's attempts to provide a variety of entertainment and to encourage new American playwrights.

In the collection are over two-dozen Living Newspapers, among them the well-known New York City productions — *Triple-A Plowed Under, 1935, Injunction Granted, Power,* and *One-Third of a Nation* — and also many unproduced scripts on topics such as soil conservation, the timber and cotton industries, consumer co-operatives, socialized medicine, and land rights in California. Many of these, including one on Afro-American history, *Liberty Deferred* by Abram Hill and John Silvera, were previously thought lost. A list of Living Newspapers with brief annotations is available.

Some scripts are of original plays with strong social or political positions. These support FTP Director Hallie Flanagan's claim in *Arena* that "the theatre must become conscious of the implications of the changing social order, or the changing social order will ignore, and rightly, the implications of the theatre." Examples are the scripts for FTP productions of *Chalk Dust* by Harold Clarke and Maxwell Nurnberg, *Life and Death of an American* by George Sklar, *If Ye Break Faith* by Maria Coxe, *Class of '29* by Orrie Lashin and Milo Hastings, *Battle Hymn* by Michael Gold and Michael Blankfort, and *Created Equal* by John Hunter Booth. The Federal Theatre offered unusual encouragement for authors who wrote on the political issues of especial importance in the late 1930s, specifically Negro rights, labor rights, and the rise of fascism. *It Can't Happen Here* by Sinclair Lewis is probably the best-known of the antifascist plays, followed by *On The Rocks* by George Bernard Shaw, but there are a number of other powerful antifascist scripts including *Professor Mamlock* by Friedrich Wolf, *The Mirror Crack'd* by John Crosby, and *Day is Darkness* by George Foss. Important black plays in the collection include *The Trial of Dr. Beck* by Hughes Allison, *Trilogy in Black* by Ward Courtney, *Big White Fog* by Theodore Ward, *Turpentine* by J. A. "Gus" Smith and Peter Morrell, *The Natural Man* by Theodore Browne, and *Haiti* by William DuBois. (A list of holdings of black FTP plays is available.) Among the labor plays are *The Cradle Will Rock* by Marc Blitzstein, *They Too Arise* by Arthur Miller, *A Time to Remember* by Marie Baumer, *Please Communicate* by Ettora Rella, *See How They Run* by George Savage, *The Lonely Man* by Howard Koch, and *$595 FOB* by George Corey.

Not all of the plays in the collection are topical; in fact, only about 10 percent of the Federal Theatre productions were social plays. There were many productions (for which there are scripts in the collection) of Shakespeare and modern classics by Henrik Ibsen, George Bernard Shaw, and Eugene O'Neill. There were comedies, like *Help Yourself* by Paul Vulpius and *Horse Eats Hat* written by Eugene Labiche and adapted by Edwin Denby and Orson Welles.

Melodramas, musicals, and mysteries were also Federal Theatre staples. The Los Angeles project used its many unemployed vaudevillians in a series of musical revues. Scripts of these shows include *Follow the Parade, Ready! Aim! Fire!* and *Revue of Reviews,* all by Gene Stone and Jack Robinson. Some of these productions were modified and performed by the Tampa unit, which also produced its own musical, *Television? A Musical Revue.* Chicago, with *O Say Can You Sing,* and New York City, with *Sing For Your Supper,* produced similar musical revues with the WPA as their topic. (Some straight stage plays were also written about the WPA, including *W-atch P-rosperity A-rise* by Bernard Ferrey, *Ten Million* by William Blake and *Code for Actors.*) Since many of the vaudevillians were so specialized and retraining seemed unlikely, some shows were pure revivals of vaudeville acts. Some of their sketches and dialogues have been preserved in script form. Examples are *Hamburger Hanna, Clothes Make the Man, De High Cost O'Chicken,* and *An Italian's View of the Labor Question.*

Many scripts reflect the Federal Theatre Project's attempts to broaden the theatrical audience. Children, youth in CCC camps and foreign-language communities were all important constituents of the Federal Theatre audience. There are scripts in French, German, Italian, Russian, Spanish, and Yiddish. Some are translations of American plays; for instance *It Can't Happen Here* in German, Italian, and Yiddish. Other scripts are of plays originally written in a foreign language.

Most major cities had Federal Theatre children's units that produced plays which attracted both youths and adults. Many of the scripts are dramatic versions of well-known stories like *Pinocchio, Cinderella, Rip Van Winkle, The Emperor's New Clothes,* and *Treasure Island.* There are also original children's plays, the most famous being the controversial *The Revolt of the Beavers* by Oscar Saul and Louis Lantz, which was charged with being a Marxist *Mother Goose.* Saul and Lantz also wrote a children's Living Newspaper on aviation titled *Flight.*

Marionette scripts are a category closely related to children's drama but during the 1930s frequently aimed at adult audiences as well. In New York City, Remo Bufano was in charge of the marionette unit, and scripts for his productions of *Orlando Furioso* and *Treasure*

Island are in the collection. His San Francisco counterpart was Ralph Chessé, whose scripts for *Alice in Wonderland, Hansel and Gretel,* and *The Jewel Tree* are also in the collection along with marionette scripts by Ruth Fenisong, Munro Leaf, and Robert Larson. Some marionette scripts, like *Don Quixote* and *Joseph and His Brothers* (by the Vagabond Puppeteers of the Oklahoma FTP), have set and costume drawings interspersed throughout the script.

In order to achieve such breadth in its script offerings, the Federal Theatre Project turned to all possible sources. They copied scripts from anthologies and subscribed to a variety of play distributors — French's, Ingram Productions, Plays-of-the-Month, and the Catholic Foreign Mission Plays were among the largest suppliers of scripts for Federal Theatre. The FTP also copied scripts from theatrical journals like *New Theatre* and *Curtain Call* (Canadian), and from such unlikely nontheatrical magazines as *American Farm Bureau* and *Journal of Home Economics,* which was the source for *A Television Style Show.*

The Federal Theatre solicited manuscripts from established writers. Shaw let the Federal Theatre present the American premiere of *On the Rocks*, and both he and O'Neill waived royalty rights to their plays. Sinclair Lewis, on the other hand, let the Federal Theatre produce *It Can't Happen Here* not only because of its politics, but also because he was assured the equivalent of a five-year run at $50 a week. Many of the successful playwrights of the 1930s — notably Paul Green, Marc Connelly, Elmer Rice, and Emmet Lavery — are represented in the collection by a number of their plays.

The Federal Theatre also searched for fresh talent. It held play contests jointly with the Dramatists Guild. George Savage's *See How They Run,* the winner the first year of the contest, was produced in Seattle. It encouraged local authors to try their hand at playwriting. Betty Smith, who was part of the Carolina Playmakers, is represented by approximately a dozen scripts, including a Living Newspaper, *King Cotton.* Playwrights also were developed through writing classes conducted by Howard Koch, whose *The Lonely Man* was produced by the Chicago FTP. New plays were picked up from the little theatres and university theatres, most notably the Vassar Experimental Theatre. *American Plan* by Mary C. St. John and Hallie Flanagan, *Blocks* by Molly Day Thacher, *Question Before the House* by Doris

Yankauer and Herbert Mayer, and *My Country Right or Left* (written collectively) are just a few of the Vassar scripts in the collection. The plays were made available to the units across the nation through the Play Policy Board and National Service Bureau, which published mimeographed play lists according to topic. Sample titles of the play lists are: Anglo-Jewish Plays, Anti-War Plays, Early American Plays, Children's Plays, Negro Plays, 90 New Plays, Patriotic Plays, Rural Plays, 72 Vaudeville Sketches, Irish Plays, Old and New Spanish Plays, and Modern Continental Plays. A list of the FTP play lists is available.

After a unit chose a play, the script library would type or mimeograph copies for that particular unit. For some productions, sides were also typed up. Sides for approximately 200 plays are in the collection. They do not seem to be of any particular kind of play or come from particular units, and titles range from *Timon of Athens* to *The Mikado*.

Some of the scripts contain valuable information about a production. Stage manager's copies of scripts are filled with lighting and prop cues. Some stage managers also noted the directors' comments and warnings about tempo and the habits of various actors. Some scripts with considerable annotation are those for the Los Angeles production of *One-Third of a Nation,* the New York production of *Sing for Your Supper* and the Atlanta productions of *One More Spring* and *Journey's End.* Other plays were heavily modified for Federal Theatre production. Orson Welles' productions are the most famous examples. Scripts for his productions of *The Tragical History of Doctor Faustus, Macbeth,* and *Horse Eats Hat* are part of the collection.

Some other scripts are of significant bibliographic interest because they show a play in the process of revision. Occasionally even the title changes, as in Howard Koch's *The Grasshoppers* which becomes *The Singing and the Gold,* or Ward Courtney's *Trilogy in Black* and *Mango.* Living Newspapers would go through considerable revision while in rehearsal and then, through "edition" changes during their stage run. In the collection there are variants of most of these plays, especially the later ones, *One-Third of a Nation* and *Medicine Show* (which was in rehearsal when the FTP closed).

There is a computer list of the script titles in the collection. The printouts list the plays according to author, title, source, and type. A catalogue card describes each script copy, since some are unmarked and some are annotated.

Music. Easily 90 percent of Federal Theatre productions incorporated music in some way — either with recordings or live performers using previously published works or orginal music especially composed for a production. Music was used extensively for the obvious artistic reasons but also because it provided employment for dancers, singers, composers, arrangers, copyists, and music librarians. It also broadened the scope of work available to instrumentalists employed by the Federal Music Project. The music collection includes manuscript music, published music, and card files created and used by the Federal Theatre Project.

Twenty-seven productions are represented in the manuscript collection. Of these, 16 productions include both conductors' scores and instrumental parts, 6 include only conductors' scores, and 4 consist only of instrumental parts. The majority are ink manuscripts prepared by professional copyists; some include multiple copies of orchestral parts.

Most of these manuscripts are of original music especially composed for Federal Theatre productions. For instance, Lee Wainer's music for Living Newspaper's *One-Third of a Nation* and *Power* is included in the collection, as is the David Sheinfeld music for the Chicago and Philadelphia productions of *Spirochete.* Manuscripts for Negro drama include music by Leonard de Paur for *Haiti,* by George Couvreur for *Androcles and the Lion,* and by Jean Stor for *Noah.* The music of Lehman Engel, the renowned authority on musical theatre, is represented in four productions: *The Birds, The Emperor's New Clothes, A Hero is Born,* and *Horse Play.* The music composed by Paul Bowles for Orson Welles's *The Tragical History of Doctor Faustus* is also in the manuscript collection.

The manuscript collection also includes arrangements of previously-composed works used in Federal Theatre productions. For example, *Two-A-Day,* a history of vaudeville by Gene Stone and Jack Robinson, makes use of such familiar selections as "School Days," "Glow Worm," and "Ain't She Sweet." In New York, Ben Russak and a pool of composers arranged *The Disappointment,* a comic opera dating from 1767 and believed to be the first known performance in 1937.

In addition to the music manuscripts used in productions, there are four manuscripts with no known connections to Federal Theatre productions. One of these, a 12-page manuscript of a song entitled "Jobless Blues," was composed by Marc Blitzstein, who also wrote *The Cradle Will Rock*. "Historical Vaudeville" is a 23-measure song with music and lyrics by Peter Arnow, arranged by Ralph Story. The third manuscript is a fragment: a one-page pencil sketch identified only as "Negro Symphony." *Rose of Alhambra*, which has orchestral parts but no score, appears on no Federal Theatre production list and apparently was never produced. Six published songs from *Swing It* and *Sing for Your Supper* have been donated to the University. Lyrics for four songs from *O Say Can You Sing* are also part of the collection.

Master sheets prepared for photoreproduction (measuring 18 x 24") exist for two Los Angeles productions, *Two-A-Day* and *Sumurun*. Neither set is complete and neither has a score, but *Sumurun* was never produced. (*Two-A-Day* was performed in Los Angeles and San Francisco.) The photoreproduction of the orchestral parts for *Sumurun* began on June 28, 1939, only two days before Congress suspended the Federal Theatre Project. The order forms are marked in red: "Cancelled."

All music in the collection is stored in acid-free folders. Information on the music collection is listed on 5 x 8" cards. These contain basic information (production title, song title, composer, arranger and lyricist); list each folder's contents; note whether the scores are full orchestral scores or condensed scores; and list the orchestral parts. (The instrumentation for most productions is fairly standard theatre orchestra instrumentation; however, no string instruments are scored in *Doctor Faustus, Horse Play, One-Third of a Nation,* and *Power.*)

The University also has the Federal Theatre Project Music Library catalogue cards and portions of the collection of published music. Consisting of approximately 1,000 pieces of published sheet music and 350 song and choral books, the Music Library evidently kept music on file for possible future use. The music covers are stamped, variously: "Library, Bureau of Research and Publication, Federal Theatre Project, W.P.A."; "Library, Play Bureau, Federal Theatre Project, W.P.A."; and "Play Bureau, Music Library, Federal Theatre Project, 303 West 42nd St."

Over 7,000 5 x 8" cards cataloguing this music are filed in three separate files: Songs as to Type, grouping titles under such headings as badinage, dramatic, hillbilly, lullaby, and patriotic; Songs as to Kind, classifying music under such divisions as cantatas, masses, musical revues, and operettas; and Songs—Their Publishers, filing titles alphabetically under publishers.

Each card contains basic information (title, publisher, and whether a score is piano, vocal, or instrumental), a classification checklist (the categories being classical, semiclassical, educational, sacred, popular, dance, and incidental), and a review of the composition. The reviews are brief, typewritten descriptions and evaluations of the music recommending or rejecting it for possible use.

Two other music files in the collection are not related to the Music Library or its files but are related to the Federal Theatre Project. Nearly 4,000 5 x 8" cards are filed in Songs Used on Federal Theatre Projects and nearly 7,000 are filed in Songs for Plays by State. The files list the published music used by Federal Theatre units in their productions. The Songs for Plays by State files also include entries for vaudeville units, variety troupes, Yiddish theatre, the Florida Marionette unit, the Negro Floating Ensemble, the Dance Theatre Project, and the Federal Theatre of the Air. Over 300 specific production titles are listed representing nearly 500 actual productions.

Other possible sources of information about FTP music include the oral histories and production notebooks. There are oral history interviews with ten Federal Theatre composers, including Virgil Thomson, Lehman Engel, and Earl Robinson. These provide unique personal details. For instance, Lehman Engel confides that the production *The Emperor's New Clothes,* for which he composed the music in one afternoon, was mounted so widely and so frequently that ". . . I think I made about three thousand dollars out of two and a half hours of work. It was almost the best pay I ever [received] in my life." Earl Robinson, composer of the music for *Processional* (which is included in the manuscript collection) and of "Ballad For Americans" from *Sing for Your Supper,* is one of several interviewees who gives impromptu musical performances on tape.

Production notebooks are useful supplements as well, because they contain programs (which list music selections, composers, music directors and the orchestra); they often include a page labeled "Suggested Music"; they may have a music director's report; and they occasionally contain detailed notes about music composed for the production. In addition, the notebooks, like the card file labeled Songs for Plays by State, reveal information about different choices of music by different units mounting the same production. Federal Theatre Project music is also located at the National Archives and the Library of Congress.

Design Records. The extensive holdings of Federal Theatre Project set and costume designs are a particularly valuable asset because they provide the researcher a rare opportunity to document all the visual aspects of a single theatre company's production history. This type of documentation is normally difficult because stage designers usually keep their design renderings in personal collections. As a result, relevant pictorial materials are scattered and inaccessible. Only occasionally are the designs left with the producer or producing company, given to a friend, or (even less frequently) sold as works of art. Most often set and costume designs are donated to an archival institution by the artist in late career or posthumously.

Thus, the Federal Theatre Project collection is unusual because it includes designs of varying quality by a broad spectrum of designers from different regions and backgrounds for diverse stages and styles of production — but all for one producing organization. The FTP designs provide insight into a variety of approaches to stage decor in the 1930s, a time of innovation and experimentation influenced by developments in Europe and in technology. Enhancing the value of the design collection for researchers are the additional collections of technical drawings for specific productions and theatres, several set models, and actual costumes from Federal Theatre productions.

The design collection is comprised of approximately 1,900 costume designs for 178 Federal Theatre productions and 400 renderings and painter's elevations for 130 productions. The work of 90 designers and scenic artists is included. Among the designers represented in the collection are Howard Bay, Tom Adrian Cracraft, Ben Edwards, Alexander Jones, Nat Karson, Sam Leve, and Frederick Stover. The collection is dominated by designs for New York City productions, but includes significant representation from Los Angeles; also available are more limited samples of designs for productions in other cities, including Boston, Hartford, Seattle, and Tampa.

Although the Federal Theatre design collection is large, that is not to say it is complete. In some cases individual designers managed to retain their renderings despite the project's efficiency in collecting records. Several of these artists however have donated their works to the University. Additional Federal Theatre designs can be found in the National Archives Federal Theatre Collection. In instances where designs are unavailable, it is likely that they were lost or damaged during or after production, or that renderings were never made.

Costume and set designs in the collection are catalogued and stored separately. Within each genre the designs are catalogued by production title and, where records exist for more than one production of a play, subdivided by geographical location or unit. Several costume and set designs are catalogued as unidentified; this group continues to diminish, however, as staff members become more familiar with particular productions through photographs and other materials, then can make specific identification.

The designs are rendered in a variety of media, including pencil, pen and ink, pastel, and watercolor. Drawing surfaces vary as well, ranging from tracing paper to the best quality rag board. The designs also vary in artistic quality, and range from very rough thumbnail sketches to atmospheric and detailed artistic renderings. Among the full-color set renderings in the collection are Nat Karson's designs for *Horse Eats Hat* backdrops, James Morcom's designs for vaudeville backdrops, and Nelson Baumé's detailed conceptions for the long-running Los Angeles production of *Run Little Chillun.* Several scene renderings by Perry Watkins for the Lafayette Theatre and other New York productions comprise a significant segment of the collection. (During Federal Theatre, Watkins became the first black to be admitted into the scenic artists' union.) Of special interest is a series of eight thumbnail color sketches for *Go Down Moses,* the Theodore Browne play that was in rehearsal in New York when the Federal Theatre closed in June 1939.

Specific production details, not readily available from artistic renderings, are provided by the many painter's elevations, shop drawings, projection designs, and property designs which are inter-filed with the set designs. In many cases, most notably that of Marc Blitzstein's *The Cradle Will Rock,* all that exists to visually document a production are painter's elevations; two elevations for the cancelled WPA production of the Blitzstein opera are in the collection. Frequently, handwritten notes on designs provide valuable information. Such is the case with Perry Watkins' design for the cow in *Jack and the Beanstalk,* where the note states "make as many of the spots as possible of gauze or scrim for ventilation."

Costume designs also provide significant details, including such documentation as fabric swatches, price of fabric, and vendor, and approval or disapproval by a Federal Theatre administrator. Occasionally, detailed measurement charts for individual actors are attached to the designs. Although each series of costume sketches offers valuable information about the visual qualities of specific productions, several are artistically or historically significant as well. Included in this group are 17 designs by Orson Welles for his production of *The Tragical History of Doctor Faustus,* a circus costume design for trapeze artist Burt Lancaster, James Cochrane's highly stylized designs for the dance production *How Long Brethren?,* and designs for characters in the marionette show *String Fever.*

The number of costume sketches in a series varies widely. The musical extravaganza *Sing For Your Supper,* for instance, is represented by 264 designs by Mary Merrill and Alexander Jones, while only 3 are available for the "voodoo" *Macbeth.* An added dimension to the designs for *Macbeth* is provided, however, by Nat Karson's notes on designing that production. Other productions for which there is extensive representation include Alexander Jones's and Rhoda Rammelkamp's 61 designs for *Life and Death of an American,* Emile Stoner's and Robert Byrne's 49 designs for *Machine Age,* and 95 designs by Mary Merrill for the New York production of *Prologue to Glory.* Dance productions are especially well documented; available costume designs include those for *Candide, The Dance of Death, The Eternal Prodigal,* and *Immediate Comment.*

The collection of blueprints and technical drawings provides detailed drawings for individual productions, among them *Machine Age* and *Housing* (the title of many of the records for the production that later became *One-Third of a Nation*). It should be noted that technical drawings are available for a large number of Chicago productions in the production notebooks and gift collection. Blueprints for theatres include those for the WPA theatre and stage at the New York World's Fair in 1939 and for the Federal Theatre at the Golden Gate Exposition in San Francisco.

Of special interest to theatre practitioners and students are Standard Detail drawings developed by the New York technical department under the supervision of Richard Rawls. This series of eight drawings provides easily comprehensible illustrations for standard approaches to several aspects of theatre production, including sound and visual effects, special hardware and equipment, and scene painting techniques. Apparently this series was prepared for distribution to Federal Theatre units nationwide and to community and educational theatres.

Three dismantled set models are included in the collection. (They evidently were dismantled for storage some time after production.) Designer Sam Leve had donated working models for *Tobias and the Angel* and *The Cherokee Night,* productions of the teaching unit at the Provincetown Playhouse in New York. These models show how the revolving sets effectively used the limited stage space of that historic theatre.

Just as design renderings are not maintained as historical collections, such stage artifacts as costumes, properties, and equipment are usually dispersed following a produciton. The Federal Theatre Project accumulated thousands of costumes during its four-year lifetime, but these were apparently distributed to educational and other institutions when the project closed. Eight pieces of Federal Theatre costuming were located at Longwood College in Virginia and were then donated to the collection at George Mason University for preservation. Authenticity of the bulk of the costumes, which were used by the New York Gilbert and Sullivan unit, has been documented through photographs and names written on costume labels. Viewing the actual costumes indicates skilled workmanship and attention to detail.

The design records, which are further augmented by renderings and technical drawings in production notebooks and oral history interviews with designers and technicians, are of value to researchers studying specific productions, individual designers, or aspects of the history of stage design and technique. It is significant that the design renderings provide the most detailed information available about color used in productions, since only a few color photographs of Federal Theatre productions exist.

Researchers needing to use the design records have access through a card catalogue listing play titles, designers, specifics about the drawing, and city or production. In addition, separate indices to designs, both by play title and by designer, are available. Due to the uniqueness of the design collection and the fragility of many of the design renderings, handling of the actual designs by researchers is discouraged unless the need to view them is absolute. A slide collection of the design records is under development so that ultimately the entire collection will be accessible in slide form.

Photographs. The Federal Theatre Project photograph collection offers a comprehensive visual representation of an exciting and innovative period in American theatre. Although the photographs were meant to document the productions and activities of the project rather than to be art forms, they nevertheless manage to capture the spirit and energy with which the project sought to entertain its vast audience, the American public. The production shots of actors on stage are mostly stiffly posed because the camera equipment was heavy and not readily maneuverable and the film was slow; the few action shots attempted are usually blurred. Despite these drawbacks, the photos seem to convey an enthusiasm and a sense of accomplishment which often eluded theatrical photographs of that time.

The collection at the University consists of approximately 40,000 photographs. Over 1,000 productions are documented with pictures of rehearsals, backstage activity, performances, set designs and construction, costumes, theatres, and audiences. Some of these pictures show how different cities staged and produced the same play. For example, photos of the Living Newspaper *Power*, taken from productions in New York, Seattle, and San Francisco, allow researchers to compare the various staging techniques used by the three units to make that production come alive for their differing audiences.

Other photographs document the wide range of innovative techniques that were used in the many FTP-sponsored experimental productions. Halsted Welles's stark production of *Murder in the Cathedral;* Joseph Lentz's provocative set for the Atlanta production of *Altars of Steel;* Charles Freeman's epic staging of George Sklar's *Life and Death of an American;* and the Orson Welles/John Houseman productions of *Macbeth* with its voodoo men, *The Tragical History of Doctor Faustus* with its extended stage and lack of scenery, and *Horse Eats Hat* with its chase on roller skates come alive through the eye of the Federal Theatre camera. Equally fascinating are photographs which verify the in-depth research required for the Living Newspaper productions. Shots of actual tenement rooms, stairwells, and alleys were used to provide the background necessary for Howard Bay's realistic set in the New York City production of *One-Third of a Nation.*

Many of the production shots, and some publicity and candid shots as well, show celebrities. Some are people of importance in the 1930s; others are figures who achieved celebrity later. The file on FTP's National Director Hallie Flanagan shows her giving a speech into a radio microphone and attending a Living Newspaper performance with Harry Hopkins. It also shows her affectinately touching the arm of her husband, Philip Davis. Orson Welles — resplendent in a three-piece white linen suit — appears in numerous photographs. In some, he confers with John Houseman; in others he directs his actors Joseph Cotten and Arlene Francis. He wears a moustache and smokes an impressive cigar, evidently trying very hard to look older than his twenty-one years. He is also shown in costume and heavy make-up as the magnificent Doctor Faustus. Circus photos contain a promotional shot of Babe Ruth surrounded by dignitaries. Eleanor Roosevelt poses in attendance at a play in Indiana, as well as at the New York opening of the "swing" *Mikado,* where she smiles politely at the small, bowing figure of Mayor Fiorello La Guardia. In other photos, Joseph Cotten swings from a chandelier during a rehearsal of *Horse Eats Hat;* Will Geer is deep in discussion over the script of *It Can't Happen Here;* Sam Leve stands before one of his set models for a New York teaching production; and a very young E. G. Marshall, listed as Everett Marshall, stares seriously into the camera (Marshall's photo was discovered among a set of mug shots — taken in New York — of people who had passed the Qualification Board's requirements for work on the project.)

Many other aspects of the Federal Theatre are preserved with photos. Audience shots abound: people milling before a portable stage in a New York City park; children sitting on their parents' laps, enthralled by a performance; young boys hanging from a street light to watch the circus parade go by. Festivals and pageants are recorded, as are publicity displays and gimmicks. One entire section is devoted to the New York unit's circus, and includes shots of clowns, dancing bears, tightrope walkers, Japino (the famous elephant on relief), and a very young triple-horizontal bar performer, Burt Lancaster. Well-documented is the open-air theatre which the FTP built for San Francisco's 1939 Golden Gate Exposition on Treasure Island. Photos chronicle the construction of the theatre building and continue through to its grand opening where Hallie Flanagan is shown buying the first ticket.

Many photographs document the making of marionettes and puppets for various units across the country, with special emphasis on New York and Los Angeles. A variety of management and office personnel appear as well, from the managing director of the circus to the manuscript typists in Los Angeles. The radio units of New York, Connecticut, and Seattle are represented. Portraits of vaudeville performers are plentiful: some of jugglers, singers, and hoofers long past their prime, others of young performers eager to continue prematurely aborted careers. (Several prints are clearly studio-made publicity stills, probably submitted with applications for relief work.)

These miscellaneous photographs effectively capture the attempt to make the project a "people's theatre." They portray the myriad activities that took place behind the stage while giving a glimpse of the people who came to watch and appreciate.

Although most of the photographs are black and white glossies of standard sizes, there are a number of unusual pieces in the collection. In 1939, over 200 color slides were taken in several units along the East Coast (although apparently not in New York) for *Pinocchio, One-Third of a Nation, Lucy Stone,* and other productions. Boston's *Lucy Stone* and *Big Blow* are accompanied by a typed narrative. Because the slides were stored in closed containers there is still some color in the film, but unfortunately that color is rapidly fading. There are ten color transparencies (probably Kodachrome) from New York, taken of *Bassa Moona, It Can't Happen Here,* and *The Sun and I.* The color on these is remarkably well-preserved, as is that of the only color prints in the entire collection, two carbro color prints of New York's *The Sun and I.* These color images are of particular importance because, except for the designs, they offer the only color visuals of Federal Theatre productions.

There is also a box of 14 black and white glass lantern slides used during the production of the Living Newspaper *Injunction Granted.* Several of these are broken and cannot be mended safely. The most unusual items are four mural photographs from the San Francisco productions *Run Little Chillun, The Sun and I, Murder in the Cathedral* and *The Warrior's Husband.* The sizes of these vary from 66 x 21" to 48 x 21". They are rolled up and have slightly tattered edges but otherwise are in good condition.

Besides the photographs in the files, numerous photos are included in the production notebooks. Usually they are reprints of originals contained in the regular file but occasionally are one of a kind.

In addition to the photographs there are 9,000 negatives from the New York City FTP units. Prints were on file for approximately half of them and are being made from a selection of the rest. The negatives reveal the eclectic choice of subjects covered by the New York photographers. Included are numerous publicity displays in neighborhood stores which advertised Federal Theatre-sponsored contests and announced appearances of the Caravan Theatre and the circus. A series on a Federal Art Exhibit shows large promotional displays from all the WPA arts projects. The photos include Art Project paintings and murals, a display of "Who's Who in the New York Zoo" by the Writer's Project, a selection of musical instruments provided by the Music Project for children to try out, and a well-attended puppet show presented by the Federal Theatre Project. Another series of over 100 negatives details the workings, services and patients of a large modern hospital.

Perhaps the most fascinating negatives document various ethnic groups and their neighborhoods. A series on streets in Harlem in en titled "Harlem Holiday." A collection of ethnic studies, "Foreign Types," goes into the work places of a Spanish printer, an Italian fishmonger and a German butcher, to name but a few. The negatives also record the busy street life of a Jewish community, where an elderly Orthodox man buys a cigar at a newstand and an old woman sells pretzels from her curbside stand.

Also of interest are negatives of a large number of newspaper reviews covering dramatic, variety, and caravan productions as well as schedules and reviews of the Federal Theatre radio shows. This variety of images provides researchers with a more complete sense of the varied concerns and activties of the WPA arts projects.

Another part of the Federal Theatre Project collection which is closely related to the photographs is the administrative records from the New York photography department. These records range from inventory lists of photographic supplies and a chart of Sonochrome positive film tints to the personnel files of the photographers. There are requests to the trucking department for trucks to carry photographic equipment to various theatres, reports on missing equipment, work orders, transportation receipts, and a timekeeping manual. Included in this material, although not directly related to the photo department, is an incomplete list of New York actors, which gives their ages and a two- or three-word description of their expertise and experience. There is also a clipping of a *Sunday Mirror Magazine* article dated September 25, 1938 about the filming of the movie *One-Third of a Nation,* which was taken from the Federal Theatre Living Newspaper play of the same name.

The memos and procedures recorded in these materials track the journey of the project from 1936 until the final days. There are letters from George Kondolf, the director of the New York project, with retrenchment orders following severe cutbacks of money and personnel in 1937. There is a list of rehearsal schedules beginning February 1938, the final one optimistically dated for the week ending July 5, 1939. A poignant file dated June 26, 1939 lists the names of 100 actors who were applying for work with the Qualification Review Board. There is a detailed dummy of a pictorial record book made in 1937, which outlined the activities of the New York project up to that time. (The actual finished scrapbook is also in the collection.)

Two boxes of records follow the careers of the photographic personnel from the day they applied for work, through their week-to-week assignments and includes records of their accidents and sick-leaves. There is even an interchange of letters between Richard Rose, the photographic supervisor, and one of the photographers, written to and from a hospital bed. Education and experience forms show that the photographers came from varied backgrounds. Some had college educations while others never finished high school. Several were born in New York and New Jersey, but one man came from the Virgin Islands, another from Kansas, and three from Russia. Nothing in the personnel files is dated later than June 22, 1939. One interdepartmental memo to Rose captures the sense of pressure that must have been felt throughout the project a good deal of the time. Dated May 31, 1938, it accompanies a newspaper photo of a group of delighted children watching a puppet show in Richmond, Virginia. The brief handwritten message conveys the feelings which often prevailed: "If you could get something like this once in a while maybe we'd be off the rocks."

All photographs are available for viewing by researchers. (Duplicates of portraits have been put into a separate portrait file for easy access.) Fortunately, there are a large number of duplicate photos which are used whenever possible to preserve a designated primary file. There are plans to make photocopies of the most heavily used photographs to allow researchers to study the images without fear of damaging the original material. A card catalogue filed by production title lists the number of photographs for each production and, whenever possible, gives the names of the people represented. Cross references direct the researcher to one-of-a-kind photographs in the production notebooks and gift collections. Photocopies and prints of all photographs can be made for a fee. An additional collection of 14,000 photos — many of which are duplicates of those in the University's collection — is at the National Archives.

Promotional Art. The Federal Theatre Project promotional art in the collection offers researchers a wealth of informative visual materials. The collection includes approximately 1,000 FTP posters for 333 theatrical productions and smaller numbers of billboard sheets, heralds, and advertising mats.

The thousand or so posters are the legacy of artists working in Works Progress Administration (WPA) Federal Art Project (FAP) poster divisions, which produced advertising for all WPA projects as well as for some other government offices. In some cities the theatre posters were made by artists who were employed directly by the Federal Theatre Project.

Poster design in America appears to have blossomed with the formation of the Federal Art Project. With the help of the silk-screen process and government support, artists and craftsmen were able both to improve technique and reach a wider audience, as evidenced by the Federal Theatre Project collection. Some of the posters for the Federal Theatre were handmade; some came out of assembly lines in which each worker added a color or piece of design; and some were the work of whole silk-screen departments designed to reproduce posters in quantity. Designs improved with experience, so that at one point Ralph Graham, supervisor of applied arts on the Chicago Federal Art Project, could claim the posters were technically comparable to any in America or Europe. Preliminary examination of the collection at George Mason has revealed the use of three printing processes. Roughly half of the posters are silk-screened; the rest are printed by offset lithography or by letterpress. The WPA projects seem to have created the bulk of the silk-screen products; private printing companies produced the rest, particularly the type-oriented posters, using offset lithography or letterpress. A few posters appear to have been silk-screened by the Federal Art Project, then sent to private printers for text material.

Trying to determine who did what is complicated by the fact that WPA project designations were not consistent. For example, posters in the collection are ascribed to WPA Federal Art Project, Federal Art Project, Poster Division Federal Theatre Project, Poster Division, Federal Theatre Poster Department, and Exploitation and Advertising Department Poster Division. More comprehensive examination may explain the discrepancies. Perhaps the Federal Theatre Project's poster division was established independently of, prior to, or after the Federal Art Project's poster division; or perhaps the various poster divisions merely went by different names in different cities.

There is also no clear-cut identification of the individual poster artists. The signature "Halls" appears on a few of the finest silk-screened posters, including *Androcles and the Lion, Big Blow, A Hero is Born,* and *Processional.* Other signatures include "Herzoy" on the *Prologue to Glory* poster, "Pratt" on *The Dictator,* "Burroughs" on *Trojan Incident,* "Leon Carlin" on *One-Third of a Nation* (the Philadelphia production), and double "h" initials on *The Case of Philip Lawrence* posters.

The WPA project posters are, in general, more artistic than the posters produced by private printing companies. Generally, they are silk-screened in three to eight colors with the design material covering a major portion of the surface and the printed material (theatre, dates, price) appearing at the top and bottom. Examples of posters exhibiting the best color coordination, artistic design, and production quality are the Federal Art Project and Federal Theatre Project posters for *Battle Hymn, The Case of Philip Lawrence, The Tragical History of Doctor Faustus, Haiti, Prologue to Glory,* and *Sing for*

Your Supper, to mention a few. Often the most dynamic posters advertise children's shows, such as *Flight, Horse Play, Pinocchio,* and *Treasure Island.* Other examples of good design and color are four small (8½ x 10") elegant models for posters for the Youth Theatre of Ohio's shows: *A Christmas Carol, The Emperor's New Clothes, The Ivory Door* and *Shepherd in the Distance.*

Some design images, like the cog wheel or the farm worker, appear frequently; the posters could be an important resource for the study of popular design and iconography in the 1930s. In addition, poster texts occasionally can provide valuable information about traveling productions or about co-sponsoring groups. For example, a poster for the Boston production of *Juan Jose* reveals that the production was co-sponsored by the Benito Mussolini Citizens Club.

About 20 posters are hand-lettered and used photographs for their images. They come primarily from Los Angeles, where they were used to show Federal Theatre Project productivity and range of offerings, and New York City, where they advertised a classic drama in the high school series. Photographs were also used on 12 poster boards (9" x 4') which picture scenes from the Living Newspapers, *It Can't Happen Here* and other productions from around the nation. All six photos on one of these boards are of Federal Theatre audiences — children and adults, indoors, and outdoors. These poster boards might have been used for theatre lobby displays.

The posters at the University represent 65 cities and eighteen states. The best represented regions include: New York State (posters for 138 productions), California (posters for 85 productions), Massachusetts (posters for 37 productions), and Illinois (posters for 29 productions). For some productions, only one poster from one city exists; for many productions there are several posters from several cities (e.g., *It Can't Happen Here:* 57 from 11 cities). The collection includes posters for plays produced from 1936 to 1939 by all Federal Theatre units (Negro, Dance, Marionette, etc.) A smaller collection of about 50 posters, mostly duplicates, is located in the Poster Division of the Library of Congress. A list of these posters, which come from Illinois, Iowa, New York, and Ohio, is available. Posters have been catalogued by production title and filed. To assist the researcher in retrieval, a shelf list is available with the number of posters per production, city, theatre, and dates.

Related to the poster collection are the small collections of heralds, billboard sheets, and advertising mats. Like the posters, they advertise a variety of Federal Theatre productions, often repeating images used in the posters. For example, the heralds for *Horse Eats Hat* and *Awake and Sing* repeat poster images. Some of this artwork, however, is for productions not represented in the poster collections. For instance, the billboard sheets for *Run Little Chillun* and *African Vineyard,* which are among the most striking in color and design, have no comparable poster. Individually these items provide valuable production information; collectively they offer glimpses into the Federal Theatre Project's advertising techniques and, more generally, commercial design in the thirties.

The heralds (8½ x 11" or 8½ x 14" paper advertisements) in the collection promote approximately 150 different performances. Most are for New York City productions, primarily for the suitcase or community theatre. These productions had limited runs at local theatres or halls, so heralds replaced posters as the main form of advertising. They serve as a valuable record of these spot bookings.

Generally, the heralds were produced by mimeograph and a few of the original zinc plates are in the collection. Most of the mimeographed heralds have some cartoon sketch along with details of time and place. The herald for *The Cradle Will Rock* includes, on its reverse, part of the musical score of the theme song. For some of the large New York City shows like *Prologue to Glory* and *Sing for Your Supper,* the Publications Division of the Federal Theatre printed the herald, using a linoleum or wood block to produce an image comparable to those in the posters. (Some of these blocks are also in the collection, including those for the "swing" *Mikado* and *Sing for Your Supper,* as well as some for unidentified plays.) The herald images for *Life and Death of an American* and *Androcles and the Lion* rank with the best of the poster art. All of the printed heralds are in one color, except for *Big Blow* and *Haiti,* which have their titles printed in red, and *Pinocchio,* which was printed in four colors. (The *Pinocchio* herald also features an "FW" initialed drawing that is also used in some of the posters.) A list of the heralds is available, providing the name of the production and the theatre.

The billboard sheets vary considerably in size and format. Some are the size of the cardboard posters and appear to be sketches or models for the actual billboards, which are three, six, or nine panels large. Most are painted with large bold lettering and simple line drawings. Many are in delicate condition, because they have been folded for over 40 years and the paper has occasionally stuck together or torn along the creases. Eventually slides will be made to preserve the originals and to simplify reference. A basic card file of the billboard sheets has been made. Approximately 200 plays are represented, with Los Angeles productions predominating.

Of all the promotional art in the collection, the most recently acquired are the Federal Theatre Project advertising mats — cardboard plates used in newspaper ads. These were acquired from the National Archives in July 1979. They range from reproductions of photos to simple announcements of title, place, and time. Plans call for them to be more thoroughly identified.

Publicity Records. Publicity records were usually generated by press agents assigned to a production by the New York Federal Theatre Project's Department of Information. The agents filed reports, stories, press releases, and statistics. This background material is generally more interesting and insightful than the official news release that resulted. There are, for example, on-the-spot reports of rehearsals in the children's unit as well as reports on FTP internal politics. The press agent was also usually responsible for program notes which provided brief biographies of the principal actors, the director, designer, and composer. Detailed reports, press releases, and program notes are available for such major New York City productions as *Androcles and the Lion, No More Peace, On the Rocks, Processional, Professor Mamlock* and *Sing for Your Supper.* The reports of the smaller local units were not as detailed, generally taking the form of weekly schedules, but they provide some basic information about the productions. Some local units also developed informational material for productions touring area schools.

Production Notebooks. Exactly how did each Federal Theatre play grow from a script and actors to a stage production? The collection's 774 production notebooks help to answer that question.

During the Federal Theatre's operation, a notebook of each play production was filed with the National Service Bureau in New York City. (The bureau was the central recordkeeping office for the FTP.) Most of these notebooks — bound and unbound — are now in the collection at George Mason University. (Duplicates and some unique copies are in the National Archives.) In many cases there are several production notebooks for one play title, since each city in which it was produced would prepare a notebook. For instance, there are 11 production notebooks for *It Can't Happen Here* and 13 for *Help Yourself.*

The information in each notebook varies considerably. Some notebooks contain only a synopsis of the play, a brief director's report, and perhaps a playbill or photographs. Most contain some or all of the following: costume and scene designs, light plots, floor plans, promotional materials and press notices, audience reactions, suggested music, budget information, royalty information, and supplementary data on the author and the play. The California notebooks appear to be the most carefully and completely done. The Chicago notebooks contain the best material on design and, therefore, would prove most valuable for historical reconstructions of the productions. New York City notebooks seem hurriedly done and often contain only a working script.

The materials in the notebooks provide both fact and opinion. While a play synopsis may offer a scene-by-scene account of the incidents in the play, the director's report often reflects an emotional response to the play and its production difficulties. The Los Angeles director of *Old Autumn* said of the play that "there was hardly enough entertainment value to be produced." But the San Bernadino director said: "*Old Autumn* is good theatre and will please no matter where produced." Clearly, a play's appeal could vary from place to place.

The amount of information in each category also differs widely from notebook to notebook. Those that contain costume designs may have renderings ranging from rough pencil sketches to detailed water color illustrations. The production notebook for Detroit's *The Merry Wives of Windsor,* for example, has watercolor costume design illustrations with fabric swatches to accompany them. Other notebooks just report that costumes were taken from stock or provided by the actors.

Likewise, the technical aspects of a play, detailed in the technical director's reports, range from the briefest of non-reports ("No technical difficulties encountered") to those like the one for the New York production of *A Hero Is Born,* which includes 20 pages of light plots and several more pages of scenery-hanging plots, property plots, and ground plan diagrams and blueprints. They range from technical jargon that sounds like gibberish to the layman (for example, from *Pirates of Penzance* in Cincinnati: "Open 6 blue hanging Olivets on Cyk; 2 stand Olivets; 3 special strips on ground rows; 14 hanging spots on front pipe; 6 Balcony spots"), to the kind of social commentary that can be universally appreciated. Pancho Gates, doing *Me Third* in Denver, commented on his set by noting that the play was a comedy about a family that was "the very essence of mediocre Americans who think themselves very superior because they are so conventional. . . . The Scene then would be a house like every house built by a contractor and decorated by a house painter." He considered his set "exactly right for the show, because the people who knew better got a chuckle, and the rest of the audience wanted a house like it."

The notebooks provide excellent illustrations of how production techniques varied from city to city. The photographs included in many of the notebooks are particularly useful in comparing productions, especially when a play lent itself to experimentation with sets. For example, in *One-Third of A Nation,* photos from different notebooks show sets ranging from the most impressionistic to the most realistic. Photos for the Detroit production show a set that was, as the art director described it, "a complete departure from realism." In contrast, Seattle photos depict a tenement designed with a "stark reality" approach, right down to the trash cans and clothes lines. The photos also can help a researcher visualize a play with sets that require unusual construction, like those in *The Adding Machine* or *Altars of Steel.*

The press notices and audience reactions recorded in many notebooks show public response to each play, and often throw light on the social climate in which the Federal Theatre Project operated. Press notices for any one production might range from unanimous high praise, to mixed reviews, to a consensus of dissatisfaction. When *The Birds* was put on in Roslyn, New York, one reviewer noted that "as far as we were concerned, *The Birds,* written 2,352 years ago by a Greek fellow named Aristophanes, could have been left buried another 2,352 years." A happier reviewer said, "You'll laugh at the play and you'll have a good time doing it."

The same variation in response can be seen in audience reactions. The notebook for Omaha's production of *Class of '29* quotes audience reactions ranging from "The best show in Omaha for the money" to "Why do you have so much swearing? I had hoped you would stop it."

As a whole, the production notebooks are excellent sources to use for an overall picture of a single production or for comparing and contrasting more than one production. Also, because of the technical information, they are good for revivals and for studies of stagecraft development.

A list by play title of the production notebooks is available. Each entry includes the city, theatre, and date of production. A separate card file notes which visual materials (photos, designs, plans) each notebook contains.

Radio Scripts. The Federal Theatre Radio Division (FTRD) was organized as part of the New York City Federal Theatre Project (FTP) in March, 1936. One month later the FTRD produced its first broadcasts: *Pioneers of Science* over station WHN and *The Old Theatre* (16 Shakespeare plays) over station WMCA and the Inter-city Network. (*The Old Theatre* was the first production of a series of Shakespeare plays on American radio; CBS and NBC followed suit the next year with a rival Shakespearean series.)

Personnel for the new Radio Division, including actors, writers, directors, production staff and office help, were selected from the ranks of NYC Federal Theatre units by Evan Roberts, the Division's managing director. In the next three years, the Radio Division employed an average of 150 people and presented approximately 2,000 programs annually. By January 1939, when FTRD compiled and printed the report "Story of the Federal Theatre Radio Division," 59 different series had been produced; and a coast-to-coast audience of more than ten million persons had heard weekly programs on art, history, music, health, safety and the law, and science, as well as children's shows, interviews with celebrities, plays, and more. Stage and screen celebrities often starred as guest artists. Sylvia Sidney, Cedric Hardwicke, Maurice Evans, Burgess Meredith, and Lillian Gish were guests on *Federal Theatre of the Air,* as was Orson Welles, who did selections from *Tamburlaine* and *Dr. Faustus.*

Providing the community with entertainment of cultural value was the goal of each individual production, but the Radio Division, like the Federal Theatre Project as a whole, had practical aims as well. These were to give relief to unemployed radio and theatre workers, to preserve and improve their skills, and to reestablish them in their professions. Some 50 percent of all the performers, writers, and technicians whom the division had employed as of January 1939 had found employment in private industry, often with commercial radio or the movies.

The Radio Division operated like a commercial broadcasting company, except that it lacked a line over the airwaves. Broadcasts were made possible by the donation of air time by networks and local stations. By the beginning of 1939, more than $5 million of air time had been donated for FTRD programs, exceeding the entire cost of the radio project by ten times, according to FTP documents. So successful was the division that by 1939 it had established ten affiliates (in Philadelphia, Los Angeles, San Francisco, Chicago, Seattle, Jacksonville, New Orleans, Boston, Atlanta, and Louisville). Affiliates cleared use of old series and development of new programming through Evan Roberts and the national division office in New York.

The 2,500 radio scripts in the collection represent 74 series and many single broadcasts. The collection provides a good sampling of the Federal Theatre Radio Division's productivity during its three-year existence, although almost all the scripts are for series originally produced in New York. Unlike the playscripts and production notebooks, the radio scripts contain little technical information. They do include, however, standard voice directions and sound effects cues and descriptions. In addition, they are almost always documented with information on the broadcasting station and the date, day, time, and length of broadcast. (Programs usually ranged from 15 minutes to one hour in length.) Most are clean, mimeographed copies.

In the collection are scripts for such varied series as *Women in the Making of America* and *The Story of Swing* (both 13-part series) and *This Was News*. The latter, a dramatization of newsworthy events from earliest times to the present for each calendar week, was broadcast for 33 weeks in 1938 and 1939 over WINS from 4:30 to 5:00 PM on Fridays; only seven segments are missing from the Center's collection. Of special interest are the radio adaptations of James Truslow Adams' *The Epic of America*. Adams gave the broadcasting rights for his book to the FTRD, as did Mary Roberts Rinehart for her

"Tish" stories and Paul de Kruif for his work which was turned into the *Men Against Death* series. Other holdings include *Experiments in Symphonic Drama,* the first series in which music was used as an integral part of the drama, with scripts developed for the music of Tchaikovsky, Brahms, Beethoven, and others; *Gilbert and Sullivan Light Opera,* representing their complete works performed by Federal Theatre actors; Ibsen's Plays, radio dramatizations of 12 major plays; and *Repertory Theatre of the Air,* including plays by Molière, Ibsen, Goldoni, Andreyev, Chekov, and Capek.

The Radio Division entered the educational field by providing recordings of several of its series, including *The Epic of America* and *Men Against Death,* for rebroadcast via WYNC, New York's municipal station, to almost a million students in their classrooms. Several FTRD programs were prizewinners. *The Epic of America* won the 1937-38 Women's National Radio Committee second place award for the finest series of educational value to radio listeners. The National Committee for Education by Radio awarded *Men Against Death* its second prize as best children's program of 1938-39. The first-prize winner was the 14-part series *Once Upon a Time,* dramatizations of classic children's literature. Scripts for all these series are available, plus a mimeographed compilation of press releases regarding *Once Upon a Time.*

In addition to scripts for series, there are several scripts for one-time programs, including two which were recorded. The first is FTP National Director Hallie Flanagan's talk, "Federal Theatre," which was broadcast on March 24, 1939 in New York and in London via CBS shortwave transmitter to the BBC. It was a 15-minute summary of the work of the Federal Theatre Project and all its "arms" — the Music, Art, and Writers Projects. The second is "No Help Wanted," a docu-drama about the WPA, written and directed by William Robson for broadcast by the BBC. A cassette copy of the transcription has been donated by Robson, whose recollections of the FTRD and the radio industry during the 1930s are included in the oral history collection.

Aside from its value to researchers studying the Federal Theatre and its Radio Division specifically, the radio script collection provides information on early radio techniques and a good means for studying audience interests of the time. Moreover, scripts for documentary and interview programs include information on specific subjects. For instance, the series *Exploring the Seven Arts,* a 15-minute evening program broadcast over WQXR in New York City, includes interviews with dancer-choreographer Doris Humphrey, writer-editor Clifton Fadiman, and theatre critic-historian John Gassner. Recreation of FTRD scripts for Broadcast today is also a possibility provided by the collection.

Researchers have access to the radio scripts through computer printouts, which provide access to the scripts by author, script, title, series title, station, source, personnel, date, and running length.

Summaries of several FTRD series have been completed by graduate students working with the collection. The programs included in this study are *A Cappella in Bronze,* a series of 15-minute programs about blacks and their traditions in the Old South; *Backstage Interviews,* a series of 15- and 30-minute programs promoting Federal Theatre stage productions; *Exploring the Arts and Sciences,* a series of talks by specialists in their fields; *Exploring the Seven Arts,* a series comprised of interviews and talks by guest artists and critics; *Their Greatest Stories,* a 28-part series of short story dramatizations; *Tish,* based on the Mary Roberts Rinehart stories; and *Women in the Making of America,* six 30-minute programs about women's historical and traditional roles in America.

The collection of radio scripts is augmented by the collection at the National Archives. Roughly a dozen of the scripts held by the National Archives are not available at George Mason University.

Nonarchival Materials. The University continually works to expand the effectiveness of the Federal Theatre Project archival collection. An adjunct collection had been developed consisting of books, magazines, articles, speeches, clippings, and unpublished research on the Federal Theatre Project, New Deal culture, and the 1930s and arts administration. Production records from modern performing and broadcasting companies who have utilized FTP materials in their productions are exciting documents for researchers who come to the University. Documents from courses, seminars, conferences, and other academic research activities are also a part of this collection. In addition to the actual materials, references to materials are collected for a master bibliography which is to be published in the future. Also, oral and video histories have been recorded.

Research on the Federal Theatre Project has been a very valuable kind of acquisition. Many published works have been acquired both on the project and on such related topics as American and European drama between the World Wars, the other WPA arts projects, and New Deal social and political history. Special attention has been paid to acquiring hard-to-find works from the period such as Robert Blake's *Awakening of the American Theatre,* Willson Whitman's *Bread and Circuses,* and FTP Director Hallie Flanagan's *Shifting Scenes,* as well as plays by authors of the period such as Paul Green, George Sklar, and John Howard Lawson. There are approximately 500 volumes in the steadily growing book collection.

The theatre magazines of the period were quite lively and influential and are another important research source at the collection. There are bound volumes of *Theatre Arts* from 1919 to 1941; complete sets of *New Theatre* and *New Theatre and Film;* the first four issues of *Theatre Workshop* (five were published); an incomplete run of *Stage* from 1936 to 1941; and miscellaneous literary publications like *The Anvil* and *Literary Digest. Variety* from 1905 to 1943 is on microfilm.

Foremost among the unpublished research works which have been donated is the manuscript "Flexible Stage" by Emmet Lavery, FTP administrator and researcher for Hallie Flanagan while she wrote *Arena,* her history of the Federal Theatre Project. "Flexible Stage," written in 1940, was intended as a companion volume to *Arena* and is rich in insight and information about the Federal Theatre Project. Another manuscript donated by Max Shohet is a memoir of his experiences as a Federal Theatre press agent. It includes chapters on children's theatre, the "swing" *Mikado, Prologue to Glory,* and the FTP protests titled "Color Me Red."

The Federal Theatre has been a fruitful source of dissertation topics in a number of fields. Many of these have been purchased or donated; so have significant dissertations on related topics. Unpublished papers and speeches plus articles published in journals and magazines have also been acquired. The staff asks researchers who use the collection to send copies of their completed work.

The oral and video histories are perhaps the most adventurous materials to be collected in support of the archival records. These projects grew out of the realization, during the earliest days of the deposit of the Federal Theatre Project materials at the University, that the FTP's paper record, no matter how rich and varied, should not be the exclusive source of insights and information about the Project. It was recognized then that to study the Federal Theatre in the broadest possible aesthetic, social, and political contexts the administrative records, research materials, readers' reports, audience surveys, designs, correspondence, and scripts needed to be supplemented with the kinds of information that could be gathered in interviews.

Much of the work and ideas of the New Deal era in general and the Federal Arts Projects in particular had for years been suppressed or discredited, due in large part to McCarthyism. However, the pioneering work done in New Deal culture during the sixties and seventies by Warren Susman, Jane deHart Mathews, Francis O'Connor, and Richard McKinzie renewed faith in the value of New Deal products and ideas. Their work gave support to the view of the staff at the FTP collection that former Federal Theatre participants, if they could be located and interviewed, would be contributing vital information about a significant historical period.

The staff further believed, as was expressed by the authors of *Amoskeag: Life and Work in an American Factory City* (Tamara Hareven and Randolph Langenback, New York: Pantheon Books, 1978) that oral history was "not merely the facts that people remember but how they remember them in the way they do." Therefore, along with the goal of factfinding, an additional goal was established: to elicit the widest possible spectrum of views and experiences on the subject of the Federal Theatre. In keeping with this two-pronged goal, an open-ended questionnaire was developed, the objects of which were: to gather background information about the participants, including their previous theatre training and interests and their political involvement at the time; to elicit information about their subsequent careers — particularly to the extent that they evolved from the Federal Theatre experience; and to obtain their reactions to federal patronage in general. The soliciting of opinions and personal experience however, was not to be a substitute for, but a supplement to, well-researched inquiries about details of productions, the internal organization of the Federal Theatre Project, play selection, theatrical experimentation, and the like.

In addition to defining a policy for interviews, it was, of course, necessary to locate and contact interviewees. When the FTP materials were first being sorted and catalogued, the staff came to recognize the names of people who seemed to have played important roles in the Theatre Project — either at local or national levels — as administrators, technicians, or performers. The staff consulted theatrical directories and agents and designers' unions; placed ads in newspapers and magazines; and searched the telephone directories of major cities across the country. Dozens of letters were written to people who might have been affiliated with the Federal Theatre. By the end of the first year, there was a sizeable pool of promising interviews. The pool grew as word passed that the interviews were taking place.

As is usually the case, women were more difficult to locate, either because of married name changes, or because their careers, like those of minorities in FTP, although they were limelighted during the years of the Federal Theatre, tended to fall into obscurity when federal funding disappeared.

Since 1976, when the oral history project was initiated, the collection of interviews has grown to more than 235, not including those done on videotape. Actors, the most prominent group, include names like E. G. Marshall, Clarence Muse, and Arlene Francis. They have recalled roles, acting styles, and feuds between directors and actors. Add Bates, for example, talks about the difficulties created by the minstrel background of some of the actors in *Androcles and the Lion*:

> We had so many people that had done minstrel theatre, and all they were doing was coming forward with teeth showing. . . . It had nothing to do with the play. . . . They were just doing what they had been used to doing. . . .

Over 50 technicians and artists who contributed to design, direction, and stage management have been interviewed. From this group, which includes prominent lighting designer Abe Feder, have come many concrete details of production and style that might otherwise be lost. For instance, Frederick Stover, art director for the Los Angeles FTP unit, describes his method of training young designers:

> I would have them compete, you see, and then we would criticize a certain design . . . if it was a multi-scene play, I would want to know exactly what happens to this set so there wasn't a

lapse with the audience sitting there getting impatient. . . . I would say, "Now, you've got something there that looks very nice from your sketch. Now, it's followed immediately by another scene. What happens to this? Does some of it fly or do you use roller stages, something of that sort?" . . . We did *It Can't Happen Here* . . . and that was a dickens of a thing to do because it had so many scenes . . . we had everything except the opening act, everything planned. And finally it was written and was sent to us. And where under the sun do you suppose it was? On a hilltop at midday somewhere in Vermont. . . . That was just one of the crazy things we got ourselves into.

The next largest group of interviewees, numbering nearly 40, includes adminstrators from the national, state, and local levels of the Federal Theatre Project. Statements from this group have provided information about daily routines, hierarchical arrangements, and important relationships within the units. In one interview, Elizabeth Elson talks about her experiences in San Francisco.

The Federal Theatre Project was going very slowly in San Francisco. No one had really taken hold and she [FTP Director Hallie Flanagan] was going to appoint me District Supervisor over Northern California area . . . with the responsibility of getting the thing really off the gound. I was a stranger, I was from the East. This did not fit very well with the San Franciscans. . . .

Fewer interviews have been completed with dancers and choreographers, playwrights, musicians, marionette artists, and writers, along with Hallie Flanagan's friends, students, and family. Examples include playwrights Emmet Lavery and Norman Rosten and composers Leonard de Paur and Lehman Engel.

The reactions of most interviewees to the establishment of the collection at the University and to the opportunity to be interviewed about their experiences have been very favorable. Participants have given generously of their time and energy. Their testimony has added greatly to the store of knowledge about the Theatre Project. While often there has been corroboration of the written record, many interviewees have both challenged existing sources and provided a wealth of new information.

During the course of the interviews, some participants revealed that the Federal Theatre had been a seminal influence in their careers. E. G. Marshall comments: "I might not have made it if it hadn't been for the Federal Theatre. . . . There were others like me. . . ."

For other participants, like black playwrights Abram Hill, Theodore Ward, and Theodore Browne, the opportunity to write and have one's work produced was all too quickly snatched away when the project was closed. Abram Hill explains:

> The Federal Writers' Project went out of existence soon after the Federal Theatre. Then there were a number of us who were idle and had nothing to do in terms of theatre art and craft.

A natural outcome of a successful oral history project is the renewed sense of pride and community among the respondents. Old friends have become reacquainted — calling, writing, and visiting, even across the country. Reunions have been held, two of which formed the basis for videotaping sessions. (One was a reunion of black performers at the Henry Street Playhouse in New York; the second was a gathering of eight women dancers in Los Angeles.)

Researchers drawing on the oral history interviews at the collection have access to transcripts for those interviews which have been transcribed, and timed abstracts for those which, to date, haven't been. However, no interview is made available until the interviewee has signed a release allowing for its research use. In some cases, use of interviews has been restricted by the authors. Some, for example, choose to restrict or prohibit use of their interviews until after their death, or for a specified period of time. Transcripts are altered only by the interviewee — words deleted by the speaker are indicated by an ellipsis. If a word is substituted, the substitution is bracketed. A recent photograph and biography is requested from each interviewee and, if received, is included with the bound transcripts.

Most interviews are roughly one hour long, although some interviewees have been able to provide such a wealth of material that they have been interviewed on more than one occasion. Cassette copies of released interview tapes are available to researchers on request. All tapes are labeled with interviewee's name, interviewer's name, place, and date.

Each interview is catalogued by the name of the interviewee. Cards are marked to indicate whether the interview is released or restricted and whether it has been transcribed. The timed abstracts are cross-referenced in a subject index by personal names, locations, theatres, productions, FTP units, and general subjects such as puppetry, dance, or playwriting.

When the oral history project was begun, it was apparent to everyone concerned that videotape interviews would be an invaluable additional project. Since the interviewees were performers or people involved with performing arts, it was expected that their gestures, expressions, and poses would tell an important part of the story that was being sought; this has proven true. The videotaped interviews explore topics which involve design, dance movement, and dramatic performance, and incorporate appropriate visual materials from the collection which provide a wealth of information for scholars and other professionals.

Because of the expense, technical difficulty, and overall complexity of the videotaping process, the video history project has progressed more slowly and has been subject to more experimentation than the oral history project. The staff has experimented with the number of interviewees, ranging from one-to-one interviews such as those with stage designer Sam Leve and actress Virginia Farmer to interviews with half a dozen or more participants. The staff has varied the mix of professions, so that in one interview, all eight interviewees were dancers, while in another — a discussion following a revival of Orson Welles' "voodoo" *Macbeth* — the interviewees were a director, a playwright-actor, a publicist, and a composer-musician. Physical environments have been varied and the results analyzed. Some interviews have taken place in the informal atmosphere of the interviewee's home; others have taken place at reunions; still others, at the University. Interview techniques and technnical equipment also have been varied.

Between 1976 and 1980, ten interview sessions were completed and provide 18 hours of videotape with 27 Federal Theatre participants. Administrators, actors, directors, designers, playwrights, and musicians were interviewed. Most interviews are one to two hours long. The interview with eight dancers is an exception, consisting of five 60-minute tapes. Some tapes are black and white; others are color.

The videotapes are labeled in the same way as oral history tapes:

with the names of the interviewee and interviewer, as well as the place and date of the interview. Video history interviewees sign a release similar to that for oral history interviewees.

A list of videotapes is available, as are timed abstracts of each tape. The tapes themselves may be viewed on request.

IV. Physical and Intellectual Control of the Records

The first shipment of Federal Theatre Project records arrived at George Mason University in the fall of 1974 and shipments continued to arrive throughout 1975. These were the archival records which the Library of Congress had received shortly after the FTP closed, and which they had roughly inventoried before storage. The materials came in wooden crates left over from World War II use; they came in wooden and metal filing cabinets; they came in old metal map cases. All in all, some 300 cartons and cabinets came to the University before the transfer was completed. The containers were dusty and rusting and many of the materials packed inside had shifted in the handling process. Although the cartons were to have been tagged and aligned with the Bourne inventory described in Part II of this article (Dispersal of Federal Theatre Project Records), the materials were actually in dissarray and mismarked, if tagged at all.

After a few temporary locations had been used to receive the materials, they finally came to be located in the University library and the unpacking, cleaning, and sorting of records began in earnest. In all truth, the library staff was not happy to see this scruffy collection housed with University library material. The staff of the Research Center for the Federal Theatre Project applied a good bit of old-fashioned elbow grease to get through the grime of the years of storage, but it was certainly rewarding when they discovered that the records were in remarkably good shape and it was the containers which had taken the brunt of the abuse.

Waiting to house and protect the sorted materials were acid-free file folders, acid-free Hollinger boxes of assorted shapes and sizes and large acid-free map folders for the designs. Recently, acid-free interleaving has been used with the photographs, designs, posters, and other materials. The Library of Congress preservation staff encapsulated some of the blueprints and technical drawings for ease in handling. The University staff is now encapsulating (on three sides only) the most heavily used designs and leaves of scrapbooks. The fourth side is unsealed for several reasons: it saves labor time, the materials are not yet deacidified, and slides have not been taken of all of the items. Slides have been taken of several hundred of the visual items (posters and designs, mostly) and it is hoped that a complete slide file will be on hand for casual research, reproductions for books and articles, and for loans to other institutions. Routine processing has included the removal of rusted metal fasteners, rubber bands, strings, and similar binding problems. Documents, especially single copy scripts, sometimes were unclear carbon copies, and these have been retyped whenever possible.

Some of the items have proven too fragile (or too dangerous, as in the case of the nitrate film negatives) to handle at the University. Many of the technical drawings and multi-sheeted billboards will undergo careful handling by Library of Congress conservators. Although colors are remarkably vivid, many of the set designs on board stock did not survive the decades of being folded and have separated at the fold line (s). The most fragile and dusty materials were the Living Newspaper Morgue clippings. They number about 75,000 individual clippings from newspapers of the period, arranged by subject matter. Several experts have felt that even if the labor required to set up these clippings for microfilming were available, the resulting film image would be too dark to be easily read. When researchers express an interest in working with this material, the staff makes xerographic copies of the desired clippings. These copies are not permanent, but copying the clippings through this process using acid-free paper would ensure a lasting copy. Since this group of materials would be extraordinarily useful to many libraries and individuals and the clippings are extremely brittle now, the staff continues to consider conservation alternatives.

An early policy decision to open the collection to researchers during the sorting and inventorying period influenced the sorting patterns. It was believed that the materials being placed on permanent loan by the Library of Congress were essentially those records created from the activity of FTP productions. The staff expected to find prompt scripts, photographs, designs, and similar materials and began alerting interested researchers. To facilitate both the preliminary sorting and research activity, it was decided to organize like items together and then arrange them by production title. Since many of the productions were done by various FTP units in various cities, a refinement was added to the title as the essential arrangement unit: production title/state/city/unit. Examples of this system would include photographs from productions of *It Can't Happen Here*. They would be filed in separate folders for each production and then labeled with: *It Can't Happen Here*/California/Los Angeles/Yiddish Unit, or *It Can't Happen Here*/Florida/Tampa, or *It Can't Happen Here*/ New York/Staten Island/Portable Stage Unit. The University has photographs from 23 separate FTP productions of *It Can't Happen Here*.

Groups of materials which could be arranged in this basic manner include photograph prints, photograph negatives, set designs, costume designs, posters, production notebooks, playbills, heralds, programs, billboards, and original music. Several large groups of materials could not use this arrangement, however, including the playscript, radio script and music libraries, research files, administrative materials, and, of course, scrapbooks.

Playscripts were originally arranged by title, in support of the production materials and because authorship could not be established easily by what was recorded on the script. It was discovered that there were many duplicate script copies; each copy was numbered and placed in a separate folder; the entire collection of 5,000 scripts was placed, alphabetically by title, in Hollinger boxes. Playscript sides (copies of scripts for each character the size of half a sheet of paper and with only cue lines from other character's speeches) were collected for each title and put directly into Hollinger boxes. Radio scripts were clustered in collections of program series and then by titles, and were processed in the same manner as the playscripts although there were fewer duplicate copies in this group of materials. Music books were organized by subject, such as "Operettas," "Folk Songs," and "Children's Songs." Sheet music was alphabetized by song title. All of these materials seemed to be part of a central library from which producing units could borrow.

The most puzzling materials to sort were those records now identified as the administrative and research records. The staff researched the organizational development of the Federal Theatre Project in an attempt to organize this material by the archival principle of provenance (that is, according to the office or department responsible for the creation of the document). Some of the documents actually dealt with agency organization, but the changes were difficult to fathom. Administrators who were being contacted about the oral history program were helpful in clarifying some of the organizational chain, but it was clear to the staff that this method of arrangement would not be productive for most of the anticipated production research. Thousands of these documents began to emerge from the sorting piles, and a method — albeit a temporary one — was needed to facilitate retrieval. Documents, and sometimes series of related documents, were placed in folders. Each folder was given a consecutive number, starting with 000,001. The folder contents were then catalogued as if they were a book, with a main entry or author, document title (many times artificially constructed), added entries and subject heading entries. The format generally followed Anglo-American Cataloging Rules I and New York Public Library Theatre Collection subject headings. Once this method was initiated, nonarchival materials, such as unpublished research and journal articles, which the Research Center was receiving or locating, were added for the sake of uniform retrieval.

Now that nearly all the materials have been identified, sorted and processed, it is time to turn back to this file and reorganize it. The archival material will be removed from the file cabinets and placed, according to a more detailed arrangement, into Hollinger boxes. Each folder is currently being examined for content and placement and a new folder number and label are being made. These changes are being noted on the cards, but the cards will remain in a master file to take advantage of the flexibility a card file allows. The nonarchival materials will remain in the file cabinets and will be arranged in several new subcollections, such as published research articles, academic research, biographical files, unpublished research, and other files. The staff activity of the Research Center for the Federal Theatre Project plus the activity being generated by the new Institute on the Federal Theatre Project and New Deal Culture continually adds materials to these nonarchival files. A short period of experimentation is needed before settling on a fixed arrangement.

Materials received from the Library of Congress are stamped with an ownership mark using ink developed for this purpose by LC staff. The ink does not damage the material but for security purposes, the mark is virtually indelible. Archival items which the University receives as gifts are marked accordingly, with the name of donor added to the ownership mark. Donated materials are stored separately from the materials on deposit from LC. When this material began to arrive, specific items such as programs, photographs (loose), playscripts, designs, and other production records were removed from the donor-based collection and interfiled with the main records. In some cases, these items were filed as a separate group of records immediately following the main file of Library of Congress records. For example, the gift photographs were filed in a separate alphabet behind the main photograph files. Recently, all the interfiled gift materials have been removed and these records are grouped together in the "gifts" section of the collection. The physical location of individual items affects the finding aids and retrieval systems. A decision to restore and maintain all gifts in sequential donor files is pending.

The state of intellectual control of the records attained in the past five years is at once amazing in its proliferation and frustrating in its staff-dependent utility. For the most part, sorted materials were arranged alphabetically by designated unit (title for playscripts; title/state/city/unit for production records; subject groups for other records). Lists of the items in a group were then made by hand. Some of these lists were typed in special formats to serve as registers which the Library of Congress wishes to publish. Other lists were used as the basis of computer print-outs. In a few instances, card files of diverse sizes and formats were made.

The result of this nonsystems approach is over 75 finding aids of such diverse formats and physical sizes, that they cannot be utilized easily by staff or researchers. Most of the aids have a "yes, but" attached to their rationale and execution. Handlists work for small groups of materials, but for the large groups within the FTP records they were never quite complete and had to be retyped with the inevitable additions to an alphabetical file. Another problem affecting the lists is the lack of a central authority for personal names, agencies and titles. This not only has caused variant entries between lists, but has produced misplaced items and separated items which should have been brought together. Card files are quickly corrected in this preliminary phase of organizational work and would have greatly simplified the compilation of registers.

Computer printouts were produced along similar lines and must be redone. The printouts are difficult to read because there is no spacing between letters in the reversed personal names or within the words of the titles. The photographs, set designs and costume designs were recorded on cards because of the complexity of information required. The 5 x 8" cards were mimeographed for uniform recording of information. This information was then typed into lists called registers, but too soon to take advantage of the recently established personal name and play title authority file. Some 9,000 standard 3 x 5" catalogue cards were typed manually to produce author, title, subject, and shelf list cards for the administrative and research records. Many of these cards reflect the spelling errors and agency name and play title inaccuracies which plague the basic bibliographic system.

Registers are the staple finding aid for archival collections. The Library of Congress Manuscript Division produces published registers of selected collections to assist researchers and libraries in locating materials. As part of the deposit agreement with the University, the Library of Congress requested that registers of the FTP records be compiled for their publication program. Initial staff efforts strove to fulfill this request with lists compiled too hastily. Part of the problem of designing efficient finding aids for the FTP records is that most of the materials on deposit at the University have been separated from their provenance, which is the general way archival records are entered and listed in registers. That is, all the production notebooks are filed together, arranged alphabetically by title, but they were not produced that way. Each notebook was compiled by the local unit which mounted the production. Similarly, not all correspondence from the Western Regional Service Bureau has been grouped together and so on. The staff met with members of the LC Manuscript Division to work out modifications of the typical register format, but several problems remain and point to whether this is the best means to share information concerning the materials.

In the last two years, all inventory work has been done on standard library catalogue cards, some by hand and some typed. The formats of the cards are not uniform, but uniformity can be imposed using word processor equipment to produce whatever kind of list is needed.

Because the word processor is connected to the University computer systems, records can be corrected, added, or withdrawn without retyping the list. It will make the job of standardized and accurate bibliographic control feasible for the FTP materials.

The final group of records to come under physical and bibliographic control will be the playreaders' reports — all 50,000 of them. They are filed now in rough alphabetic order by play title. Student assistants are pulling all reports for the same play, placing them in a single acid-free folder, labeling the folder, and making a catalogue card. Carbon duplicate reports and other extraneous materials are being removed during this process. This work has signaled the time for going back over the other groups of materials for accuracy and removal of duplicate materials. Once the project to catalogue the individual playscripts (as opposed to just listing the title/author) was begun, the value of the review was clearly evident. Some plays have been found to be filed under several variant titles; scripts marked as "copy" turn out to be prompt scripts, third-draft revisions, or not really the same play at all. In the new system, all true duplicates will be removed from the main file and variant "copies" will be catalogued as originals. Part of this project is the simultaneous establishment of authority files for each title and author. As each group of materials undergoes a similar review, entries will be matched against the authority files for uniform spelling and wording.

The use of the term "finding aid" is meant in its broadest scope. Some of these useful tools locate information rather than a specific document, such as the index to the unpublished manuscript "The Flexible Stage." The series of indexes which the staff compiled for the *Federal Theatre Magazine* assists the researcher in the location of both information and visual images, and it is an especially useful supplement to the production records in the collection. Most of the finding aids, regardless of format, are meant to represent the shelf order of specific groups of documents, to include essential identifying information (such as the name of the designer for costume designs), and, in many cases, to provide additional access other than shelf order (for example, there is an index to the list of costume designs by designers and a radio script may be located by the series title, the program title, an author, key personnel, the name of a radio station, the air time or running length, or agency source of the script). In addition to the finding aids created by the University staff, the administrative and research card files created by the original FTP staff are often excellent sources of information. The combined number of finding aids in list, card, or computer printout format exceeds 125. This situation has tended to keep the researcher dependent on staff as guides throughout the entire research visit and has made mail inquiries difficult on the staff. In time, the systems approach now being applied to the documentation of the collection will yield accurate and unified finding aids, especially in formats which can be easily shared with researchers and libraries. For the present, two bibliographic coordinating projects have been initiated to alleviate problems in the full utilization of the finding aids.

The majority of researchers want to know at some point in their searches what types of documents the collection holds for a specific production. The Production Information card (a 5 x 8" mimeographed card) has been designed as a checklist for holdings on any of the 2,400 FTP productions. The top section of the card specifically identifies a production by title, author, classification, city, theatre, opening and closing dates, and number of performances. A series of checklists follow in several categories. Under production records, a check would be made if the University holds a script, designs, program, photographs, or other records. Administrative, oral history copyright, and research information checklists are also included. A researcher would be required to look the production up in the costume design file to learn how many and which designs are available, but the card serves as a guide to the basic resources. It is also a simple matter to photocopy the card for use in mail requests, and many researchers photocopy the card as a personal search record. This data file is also being used as the base for a publication about FTP productions which the University is completing for Greenwood Press. This reference tool will be a day-by-day and city-by-city listing of each FTP production from 1935 to 1939. Numerous indices will allow for access to the central listing (which will include selected holdings information) by titles, authors, city, theatre, and production type (drama, puppet, dance, etc.).

A second type of coordinating aid is the *Directory of Finding Aids*, for which work has just begun. There are two parts to the directory, a descriptive listing of each finding aid with an assigned number and a subject index. The subject index would list entries such as "playscript" followed by the name and number of each finding aid which has information on playscripts; it will also include less obvious entries, such as "actors," "budgets," and "speeches." It is hoped that this kind of tool will free the staff for more quality time with researchers and give the researcher a sense of having touched all reasonable bases during his search. Once the directory has been completed, copies may be shared with researchers and libraries who request them.

Despite the loose ends, which exist in all collections, the FTP records at George Mason have received an impressive attention to physical conservation and bibliographic detail. Many new bibliographic projects are planned and indications are that the University has no thoughts of abandoning its love affair with the Federal Theatre Project.

RESEARCH MATERIALS OF THE FEDERAL THEATRE PROJECT IN THE THEATRE COLLECTION OF THE NEW YORK PUBLIC LIBRARY AT LINCOLN CENTER

by Dorothy L. Swerdlove

The Theatre Collection of The New York Public Library has been collecting information on the Federal Theatre Project since the program's start in the mid-1930s. The material has flowed in from three major sources: newspaper and magazine articles clipped or indexed by the Theatre Collection staff as part of its normal operations; scripts, press releases and other records officially deposited in the New York Public Library by the Project administration; and gifts from private individuals. The last category ranges all the way from a few programs sent in by members of the audience to large collections of personal papers donated by people who were actively involved with the Project.

The most important private donation was the presentation to the Theatre Collection in 1964 of the personal papers of Hallie Flanagan Davis, former Director of the Federal Theatre Project. Ms. Davis' papers comprised scripts, correspondence, speeches, administrative papers, published books and articles, photographs, programs, scrapbooks, and portfolios of newspaper clippings. They represent a documented picture of the Federal Theatre Project from its inception in 1935 to its demise by act of Congress in 1939. Similar gifts, though not as large or as all-encompassing, were received from Rosamond Gilder, the estates of designers Nat Karson and Tom Adrian Cracraft, and the estate of Edward Goodman who was an important producer-director for the Project in New York. Even today, we continue to add to our store of information on the subject whenever we come across relevant items as we catalogue scrapbooks and other memorabilia in recent donations.

While a great deal of the material on the Federal Theatre Project centers around activity in New York City where the program was

Dorothy L. Swerdlove is the Curator of the Billy Rose Theatre Collection of the New York Public Library at Lincoln Center.

particularly strong, there is also information on regional tours and on local activities in other parts of the country as diverse as Chicago and Mississippi and New Hampshire. We have several volumes of monographs, many of them illustrated, which were written about the history of San Francisco theatre by the Writers' Program of the Works Progress Administration in Northern California. Subjects covered in these monographs include: famous theatrical personalities who performed in San Francisco; foreign theatre (French, German, and Italian) in the city; little theatre groups; opera, burlesque, and minstrel troupes; and theatre buildings in San Francisco.

As is well known, the Federal Theatre Project embraced a tremendous variety of public entertainment. The materials on file in the Theatre Collection document this range of activity, frequently in great detail. Our holdings include: scripts, posters, programs, photographs, original designs, financial and technical records, historical and critical research papers, guides and bibliographies, correspondence, drafts of speeches, handbills, books and periodicals, miscellaneous pamphlets and brochures, press releases, and newspaper clippings and reviews. We also have references in our catalogue to material in other divisions of The New York Public Library — e.g., the Music Division, Genealogy and Local History Division — which pertain to the Federal Theatre Project.

There are over 100 play scripts from the Project in the Theatre Collection files, including several of the innovative Living Newspaper plays: *Injunction Granted; 1935; Triple-A Plowed Under; Power;* and *One-Third of a Nation.* One script which we do not have is *Ethiopia* by Arthur Arent, which was the first offering in the Living Newspaper series. This production, which dealt with the Italian invasion of Ethiopia, was scheduled for production in early 1936 but it was canceled at the last minute under pressure from Washington because the United States was trying to maintain a position of political neutrality. However, we do have programs and reviews of the "dress rehearsal" of the production as well as several items dealing with the incidents and its effects (including the resignation of Elmer Rice as Regional Director of the FTP.) The text of *Ethiopia* was later published in *Educational Theatre Journal,* XX (March 1968) 15-31.

Many of the scripts are annotated promptbooks or "working scripts," interleaved with production photographs and ground plans.

Among our "working scripts" are: *One-Third of a Nation* and *Power,* both by Arthur Arent; *Macbeth; Hymn to the Rising Sun* and *Unto Such Glory* by Paul Green; Christopher Marlowe's *Dr. Faustus; Processional* by John Howard Lawson; *A Hero Is Born* by Theresa Helburn; and *The Emperor's New Clothes,* a children's play.

For virtually all of the plays which were produced in New York, and for many of the plays produced elsewhere in the nation, we have programs and reviews filed under the title of the play. We also have production photographs and posters for several of the presentations. The portfolios of original designs by Tom Adrian Cracraft and Nat Karson include work they did for the Project. (Mr. Karson designed the costumes and scenery for the Orson Welles *Macbeth.*) There are also four portfolios of costume and scene designs by different artists for various Federal Theatre productions which came to the Theatre Collection via the U.S. Veterans Administration — though how these designs found their way into the VA archives remains something of a mystery. One of these portfolios contains a series of scene designs by Frederick Stover for *Two-a-Day,* which celebrated the history of vaudeville in the United States.

In the field of puppetry, there are several scripts, with titles ranging from *A Christmas Carol* and *The Valiant Little Tailor* to *R.U.R.* and *Sherlock Holmes* and *Holy Night, a Miracle Play,* for many of the plays were aimed at an adult audience. Our Federal Theatre Project files in this area include: a *Bibliography of Marionette Plays;* a *Puppetry Manual; The Puppet Teaching News Bulletin;* an *Index to Puppetry,* which is a classified list of magazine articles published between 1910 and 1938; and programs, posters, and photographs for various productions.

Radio scripts form another extensive collection of material, amounting to about 1,950 pieces. Some of the scripts are episodes in a series, while others are full-length plays or documentaries. These scripts have not been fully catalogued as yet, but Donald W. Fowle of the Theatre Collection staff is coordinating our holdings with those held by the Research Center for the Federal Theatre Project at George Mason University, with a view toward eventual microfilming the combined collections.

Among the miscellaneous publications of the Project's National Service Bureau in New York City is a series of 54 play lists suggesting titles for use by various groups — children, ethnic, religious, etc. — which include information on casts, sets, playing time, source for the scripts, etc. There is also a list of 72 vaudeville sketches and a list of 56 minstrel skits recommended for use by community groups, with the same type of production information, as well as instructions for mounting pageants and similar presentations.

Of particular value to the researcher are the files of clippings and miscellaneous materials — over 100 volumes and portfolios (including 43 from Hallie Flanagan Davis) — which have been gathered from many sources. By studying performance schedules, attendance statistics, financial reports, correspondence, minutes of meetings, technical data, press releases and contemporary newspaper accounts from all over the country, one can follow the operations and problems and accomplishments of the Federal Theatre Project from beginning to end and even beyond, for its influence was felt well beyond the 1935-39 period of its formal existence. The material has been catalogued and indexed so as to give direct research access under many different headings in addition to the Federal Theatre Project *per se:* titles of plays; names of individuals; geographical breakdowns; subject headings such as "labor: stage: U.S.," "open-air performance," "circus," "Negro in the theatre," etc. In this way, the Federal Theatre Project material can be used in conjunction with other materials in our files that deal with the same person or subject.

For some research purposes, this aspect of the collection is even more important than the straightforward documentation provided for the Federal Theatre Project. If one is writing a biography of Orson Welles or Elmer Rice or Hallie Flanagan Davis, or studying the production history of a play such as *Macbeth* or *Dr. Faustus,* or looking into the background of the *New Living Newspaper* currently being presented Off-off-Broadway in New York City, or researching broader topics such as the history of black theatre in the United States or governmental support of the arts, the Federal Theatre Project forms an important segment of the story but by no means the whole history. Through the extensive indexing and cross-referencing provided in our catalogue, this information can be linked to other items in the Theatre Collection to form a comprehensive historical and critical account.

THE MUSEUM OF BROADCASTING

Introducing the Museum of Broadcasting by Robert Saudek

The Museum of Broadcasting, located at 1 East 53 Street in New York City, is the first American museum dedicated to the study and preservation of the more than fifty-year history of radio and television broadcasting. Through the cooperation of all the networks and of public broadcasting, the Museum maintains a rapidly-growing collection of significant radio and television programs from the 1920s to the present, professionally selected, catalogued, and indexed. The Museum was founded by William S. Paley, Chairman of the Board of CBS.

Visitors to the Museum of Broadcasting enjoy easy access to this collection, selecting program material from an extensive computer-generated file of index cards and then monitoring their selections at one of our custom-designed broadcast consoles. The Museum also maintains a library of rare radio scripts, as well as books and periodicals on broadcasting. During the morning, the Museum is reserved for use by classes, and lectures and seminars are arranged with colleges and universities for as many as twenty-four students at a time.

Among the items in the collection are some of the earliest broadcasts in existence. The collection contains speeches by each president of the United States since Warren G. Harding. Thirty-eight of Herbert Hoover's and Franklin D. Roosevelt's speeches from the 1932 campaign are included, as well as a full complement of Roosevelt's preserved statements, starting with one made in 1920. Rare musical, comedy, and dramatic material from the 1920s has also been acquired, including the Rhythm Boys with Paul Whiteman's orchestra, Walter Damrosch's "Music Appreciation Hour," and "Newsacting," the 1929 forerunner of the popular *March of Time* series.

Other highlights of the Museum's current radio collection are many dramatic productions from the "Columbia Workshop" and "One World Flight" series, examples of the 1937 "Shakespeare War," the

Robert Saudek is founding President of the Museum of Broadcasting.

earliest version of "Amos 'n' Andy" (1926), radio coverage of Charles Lindbergh's triumphal return to the U.S. in 1927, and a sampling of the popular comedy and musical variety programs of the 1930s and 1940s.

Many of the television programs are drawn from the first five years of network broadcasting (1948-1953). Among the "firsts" in this collection are the first transcontinental television broadcast (coverage of Truman's signing of the Japanese Peace Treaty, 1951), the first Presidential tour of the White House (Truman, 1952) and the televised Kefauver Crime Hearings of 1951. The pioneering dramatic series of the 1950s — "Studio One" and "Playhouse 90" — are represented, as are the classic comedy routines of Bert Lahr, Lucille Ball, Beatrice Lillie, and Jack Benny. The only recorded performances of Katharine Cornell are in the collection. Among broadcasts recently acquired by the Museum are the full series of "Roots I and II," "Holocaust," "The Magnificent Yankee" with the Lunts, and "Love Among the Ruins" with Hepburn and Olivier.

A visit to the Museum reveals the varied uses of the collection: a student of journalism compares the styles of reporters from Edward R. Murrow to Barbara Walters; a sociologist studies the portrayal of women in 1950s commercials; a mother shows her children Mary Martin as Peter Pan. These are just a few of the riches of five decades of American broadcasting collected, catalogued, and available to see and hear at the Museum of Broadcasting.

Annual memberships are available, affording free, priority use of the Museum's facilities. Nonmembers, admitted on a first-come, first-served basis, are requested to make a $1.50 contribution ($0.75 for children under 13).

What the Dumbwaiter Saw by Mary V. Ahern

In most museums, it is difficult to determine what particular objects or paintings in a general collection are looked at every day. Did 20 people study Picasso's *Guernica* today as they went through the Museum of Modern Art? Are more people interested in the Boucher panels than the Fragonard canvasses in the Frick Collection? I don't suppose a study like this can be made elsewhere, but at our Museum we can and do keep these statistics, which I think will be of interest in themselves to show differences in viewing attitudes over the years.

Each day we are open, the general public and members can choose to see anything from our collection. We will never have programs that are unavailable in some storage vault. Everything that is part of our collection can be on view. In the two and a half years since we opened, about 81 percent of the television collection has been viewed one or more times, and about a third of the radio collection has been replayed. So the dumbwaiter which transports the cassettes from stacks to playback screens has seen a variety of selections encompassing drama, sports, ballet, great comedians (Fred Allen, George Burns and Gracie Allen, Jimmy Durante, Beatrice Lillie, Jack Benny, Danny Kaye, Fanny Brice), historic events like the assassination of John F. Kennedy, Martin Luther King's March on Washington, and on and on. I asked the dumbwaiter what it saw on a random day — Saturday, February 10, 1979. (Remember that we are open five hours a day, Tuesdays through Saturdays.) This is what the dumbwaiter saw on that afternoon: 61 programs ranging over 39 years of broadcasting history from John F. Kennedy's discussion of his book *Why England Slept* on a 1940 radio program to 1979's "The Best of 'Saturday Night Live.' "

All Star Revue, "The Jimmy Durante Show," 4/19/52
Classic Commercials, 1948-1968
The Ed Sullivan Show, Beatles' debut, 2/9/64

Mary V. Ahern is the Curator of the Museum of Broadcasting.

Ford Star Jubilee, "Together With Music," Noel Coward and Mary Martin, 10/22/55

Producer's Showcase, "International Festival of Magic", n.d.

Playhouse 90, "The Comedian," with Mickey Rooney, 2/14/57

House Judiciary Committee Impeachment Hearings, 7/24/74

Happy Days, Premiere, 1/15/75

Address by Senator Joseph McCarthy, 11/24/53

Monty Python's Flying Circus, 10/13/74

Star Trek, Animated Version, "More Tribbles More Troubles," 10/6/73

The Best of Saturday Night Live, 1/10/79

The Edsel Show, Frank Sinatra and Bing Crosby, 10/13/57

Arthur Godfrey Time, Rehearsal for Godfrey's TV debut, 1/23/48

Tribute to Lou Gehrig, 6/3/41

Howdy Doody, 1948

The Milton Berle Show, Elvis Presley, 6/5/56

Person to Person, Frank Sinatra and Joseph N. Welch, 9/14/56

Propaganda Germany, Lord Haw Haw, 5/20/40

Propaganda Germany, "Paul Revere," 9/19/41

Propaganda Germany, Robert Best, 11/9/42

Amos 'n Andy, 9/21/49

The Guiding Light, 1/17/56

As the World Turns, 1/3/62

The Fugitive, Premiere, 9/17/63

Perry Mason, Premiere, 9/21/57

The Making of the President, 6/11/64

Camel News Caravan, with John Cameron Swayze, 9/4/50

Olympic Games, Munich, 9/10/72

Gunsmoke, Premiere, 9/10/55

CBS News Special, "Echoes of the Guns of Autumn," 9/28/75

CBS, On the Air, Pt. 1, 3/26/78

ABC Silver Anniversary, Pt. 1, 2/5/78

ABC Theatre, Mary White, Pt. 1, 11/18/77

Playhouse 90, "A Child of Our Time," 2/5/59

Twilight Zone, "Where Is Everybody?," 10/2/59

I Love Lucy, "Lucy's Italian Movie", n.d.

They've Killed President Lincoln, 2/12/71

All Star Revue, "The Jimmy Durante Show," 2/9/64

Your Show of Shows, with Sid Caesar and Imogene Coca,
    12/23/50 and 4/28/51

Playhouse 90, "Days of Wine and Roses," 10/2/58

Gene Kelly in New York, 2/14/66

Star Trek, "Where No Man Has Gone," 9/22/66

Texaco Star Theatre, 3/15/49

Stars in the Eyes, Dedication of CBS TV City, with Jack Benny,
    11/15/52

John F. Kennedy on *Why England Slept,* 1940

Churchill, "Their Finest Hour," 6/18/40

Nixon-JFK Debate #4, n.d.

World Today, 6/3/40

Chronoscope, Premiere News Show: Atomic Bomb Debate,
    6/11/51

Kovacs Unlimited, 5/28/52

CBS News Special, Report on the Cuban Missile Crisis,
    10/24/62

These 61 programs were viewed by 47 persons (some in groups of twos
and threes at the eight available consoles). With the new expansion
of public areas for viewing and listening, we will be able to accommodate up to ten times that many visitors in the same 12:00-5:00 PM
hours that we will be open.

In sum, there is an advantage to this new kind of museum of ours
because it can make everything in the collection available to the
public and members and deliver programs within minutes of the
requests.

Now I would like to look at that list of programs in a different way,
from the point of view of our selection process. I am not going to give
every citation but enough so you will see why those programs chosen
to be listened to again on that day are in our collection. Since broadcasting has covered such a wide spectrum of human performance, we
want to have in five years a stunning sample composed of 9,000 hours
which will represent the following "inner collections" among others.

I. *The high-rated collection:* On February 10 we see in this area
All Star Revue, The Ed Sullivan Show, Star Trek, Arthur God-

frey Time, Texaco Star Theatre with Milton Berle, Perry Mason, Happy Days Premiere, and I Love Lucy. (On other days, the dumbwaiter has seen the highly rated Roots, All in the Family, Mary Tyler Moore, etc.)

II. *The performing arts:* Playhouse 90's "The Days of Wine and Roses," "The Comedian," and "A Child of Our Time"; Your Show of Shows (on another day it might be Kraft Theatre, Philco, Omnibus, the Bolshoi Ballet, Baryshnikov, or "The Barretts of Wimpole Street" with Katharine Cornell).

III. *Milestones, specials and debuts in radio or TV:* the Beatles on Ed Sullivan, Gene Kelly in New York (with an appearance of the fledgling comic Woody Allen), Noel Coward's debut on Ford Star Jubilee, and the anniversary programs of CBS and ABC. (On another day, it might have been NBC's First Fifty Years or The Ford Fiftieth Anniversary Program starring Ethel Merman and Mary Martin, or the first transcontinental telecast picking up President Harry S. Truman on the West Coast.)

IV. *Children's programs:* Howdy Doody, Star Trek, Producer's Showcase Magic Shows. At another time it might be Mary Martin's *Peter Pan* or Dr. Seuss's *Grinch,* or *Tom Brown's Schooldays.*

V. *World War II collection:* The radio programs on the list include German Propaganda (Lord Haw Haw, "Paul Revere," Robert Best); Churchill's "Their Finest Hour," and the young John F. Kennedy explaining his book *Why England Slept.* (This collection will be a dominant one with the famous first-hand radio reports from Edward R. Murrow, H. V. Kaltenborn, and William L. Shirer of the main events of World War II. It of course will have many echoes in television with Holocaust, Dwight D. Eisenhower and Walter Cronkite in D-Day Plus 20 Years, Victory at Sea, etc.)

VI. *Sports:* Olympic Games of 1972 in Munich. We have a lively sports collection from Joe Louis to Muhammad Ali as well as Superbowls and other Olympic Games.

Our guidelines and goals are helpful in the selection process of trying to locate the finest, the memorable, significant, and popular because we can always fill in series in later years but we start with representation of the series first. For See It Now, we start with Murrow and Sen. Joseph McCarthy, and Danny Kaye's UNICEF Show, and The Lady from Philadelphia: Marian Anderson and a dozen others from this series; later we will want to fill in more and more of such a series and we encourage suggestions from our users. There are Program Suggestion Cards available and often we get information — the date of a program we have been searching for — which we would not otherwise have found or a correction for which we are always grateful.

I like to say that the three people who set the guidelines had 120 years of experience working in broadcasting (William S. Paley, the founder of the Museum, 50 years; Robert Saudek, 40 years; and myself with 30). That 120 years of experience was brought to bear to see that our collection would become a brilliant representation of a medium which we all respect and which we know had and has many messages to impart. We trust we will have a body of television and radio programs and coverage of historic events sufficiently worthy of our growing number of members and the public and that they, with us, will watch it grow and grow.

Using the Museum of Broadcasting's Catalogue by Douglas Gibbons

When you begin your program search at the Museum of Broadcasting, the first contact you have may be with the Museum's unique computer-generated cataloguing system. To understand how unusual this system is, we will follow the course of the program documentation from cataloguing through editing and indexing, keypunching, and proofreading, to receipt of the 4 x 6" printed catalogue cards ready for study. We will also look at typical card catalogue search techniques and see how future on-line possibilities using an in-house computer will effect searching.

The cataloguing of the collection is based on the playback of a program in its entirety ("real time") by a cataloguer. This allows the cataloguer to summarize content based on a knowledge of the complete program and not just selective skimming. After verifying the cast and production credits and the date and time of broadcast, the cataloguer's rough notes are rewritten into final summary form and given to the librarian.

The librarian edits the summary and indexes the program, providing cross-indexing approaches by accession number, series title, subtitle or episode title, network, date of broadcast, genre (e.g. news, comedy, public affairs-documentaries, drama, etc.), notable production and cast credits, and subject headings. (The subject headings are chosen from a growing alphabetical list of more than 500 topics based on Library of Congress subject headings and indicate the depth and scope of the collection.) Thus, a typical program may be indexed as many as fifteen ways.

The summaries are edited to conform to the computer format, typed on coded worksheets, and then sent to a computer service bureau for keypunching on computer cards. (All computer work is performed out-of-house.) The summaries then go from punched card to magnetic tape, producing a galley proof which is returned to the librarian for an accuracy check; the proof is approved and returned to the service bureau; and the computer prints sets of 4 x 6"

Douglas Gibbons is the Librarian of the Museum of Broadcasting.

catalogue cards which are then filed in the library's card catalogue, ready for use.

Each card reproduces its program credits, summary, and cross-indexing approaches in full, displaying one particular cross-index term on the top of the card. The cards are filed by the top line in a "dictionary" style, an arrangement that shortens the user's search time by reducing the back tracking involved with "see" and "see also" references.

Three index approaches that are filed separately are "Dates," "Radio," and "TV." These are useful for browsing, since under the first are listed all programs in the collection and under the latter two are listed all programs in a specific medium.

Most searches can be easily performed now because the collection is relatively small and requests are specific. By using just one of the many index approaches the user will immediately know whether or not the Museum has an example of the craft of Cornell or Cobb, a fondly remembered program such as *Peter Pan,* a Presidential press conference, or a treatment of the energy crisis in America.

As the collection grows, searching will become more time consuming for there will be many more programs with similarities. Even now, users wanting an overview of the Museum's holdings of broadcasts relating to the administration of President Franklin D. Roosevelt must scan several dozen catalogue cards.

In the future, as the collection and its uses grow, it may be desirable to install a computer terminal in the library. The terminal would resemble a teletype-typewriter keyboard and would have a cathode-ray tube (CRT) display unit attached for visual printout of information on a small screen. The unit could be rented at first, with the Museum's computer tape stored at an outside computer center under a time-sharing system. Eventually, a terminal might be purchased as demand and budget allow.

The user's request would be entered by typing it in computer language on the keyboard and would be simultaneously seen on the CRT display screen. The display would be checked for accuracy and then the requested information would appear within seconds. The user would have the option of obtaining a permanent visual record of the search for future use.

Creating an Exhibition at the Museum of Broadcasting

by Judith E. Schwartz

With the number of film and video archives and museums on the rise, the possibilities for new forms of interpretive exhibits also increases. The combined efforts of museologists, historians, and media specialists can produce educational experiences that reflect the best qualities of each. At the Museum of Broadcasting there exists a splendid opportunity to couple the excitement and drama of "present-tense history" with the objectivity of hindsight. The Museum's expansion will include an assortment of spaces and allow a range of situations for the presentation and explanation of the broadcasting medium to the public.

The exhibition Boxtop Treasures: The Evangelista Collection of Toys and Premiums from the Golden Age of Radio (Museum of Broadcasting, April 20-July 28, 1979) may be approached on several levels. The show combined excerpts of radio adventure programs with explanatory narration, photo panels, and the actual relics of a child's culture.

Anthony J. Evangelista, a professor of art at Kutztown State College in Pennsylvania, made available an impressive collection of the premiums given away in the 1930s through the 1950s as well as some of the beautifully crafted toys sold to fans. Little Orphan Annie, Jack Armstrong: the All-American Boy, Buck Rogers, Captain Midnight, the Tom Mix Ralston Straightshooters, Superman, the Lone Ranger, Charlie McCarthy, and Dick Tracy were represented by colorful objects selected for their visual impact and historical importance.

The toys, grouped according to program against stark black and white backdrops, could be viewed simply as enjoyable, attractive artifacts from an earlier time or from their moral and promotional perspectives. Most of the shows stressed the triumph of good over evil. While the degree of violence used to achieve that end varied,

Judith E. Schwartz, former Public Information Officer of the Museum of Broadcasting, mounted the exhibition Boxtop Treasures.

listeners were admonished to be good patriotic citizens, be helpful to parents, play fair, and keep clean. The Lone Ranger, for example, offered first-aid kits in two sizes. During World War II, children were asked to assist with the war effort through paper drives, writing letters to their fathers overseas, and supporting their radio heroes as they chased enemy spies.

Promoted even more than these positive ideals were the sponsor's products. A radio show would generally be supported by one sponsor who usually had a commercial at the beginning, the end, and sometimes in the middle of the program. As most shows ran for only fifteen minutes, advertisements for products and premiums took up at least a third of the time. Listeners had to send in a boxtop from the sponsor's product to obtain the premiums. Not only were the premiums (and sometimes the products) incorporated into the drama of the show, making them positively tantalizing, but letters often accompanied the prize, urging further purchases. Included in the exhibit with the Buck Rogers Radio Adventure Theatre was a note from Buck himself telling his "friend" to tell his or her friends how "beneficial" Cocomalt is.

The pervasive pressure of the commercials was further illustrated by the tape that accompanied the exhibit. Visitors saw a Philco cathedral radio in which the tape deck was hidden, placed in a comfortable listening area. Selections from the programs with the commercials gave a sense of the effective and insistent sales pitch as well as the dramatic techniques used in radio. The narration gave general historical background and pointed out the unique factors of each program.

The small size of the library and the total inflexibility of the lighting severely limited the structure of the exhibition. Wood and plexiglas cases placed on top of the card catalogue (which runs along the perimeter of two walls) were secured to the wall. The high-contrast photo panels functioned structurally as the rear walls of the cases, provided additional animation for the room, and acted as nonverbal labels. They used comic strips, publicity shots of the actors in costumes, and production stills as images. Their simplicity gave added force to the objects themselves. The bookcase was rearranged to create plexiglas-enclosed exhibition space. The show generated favorable press and audience response.

The traditional means of presenting video and film is to show an example of the institution's collection in a darkened auditorium. Interpretation can come in the form of thematically-grouped selections of individual programs or features. While always a good method, it does come in direct audience competition with first-run and revival movie houses and television. Still to come is another, more specialized means of displaying the Museum's audio and visual materials.

The educational goals embraced by the institution and staff, the physical and technical facilities, and the monetary resources available will affect how far the Museum will wish to guide the audience's understanding about the medium. Displaying artifacts integrated with electronics, as in Boxtop Treasures, is a possibility, though that could have been carried even further with the use of "talking labels."

An area with tremendous potential is the production of edited video tapes for exhibit purposes. Whether one is communicating the development of set and costume design or comparing the performance of different actors in the same role, video (and audio recording) offers immediate presence. This can function as a straightforward presentation of the elements, arranged and identified to aid understanding of the concept or it may be supplemented by narration or technical effects. The involvement of skilled video artists and technicians can lead not only to additional insight but other funding sources as well. And, while it may seem far-fetched, computer-generated imagery should also be considered as an exhibit tool.

The possibilities are as endless as the new technology. Instead of viewing technology as a rival of artistic purity, it should be used to strengthen the importance of the arts and as a means of reaching a greater public.

ARCHIVES OF THE MOUSE FACTORY

by David R. Smith

There are few places in the world where you can go and find someone who has not heard of Mickey Mouse or Donald Duck. Mickey Mouse's career has spanned half a century and during this time his stories have been printed in forty-five countries and in thirty-five different languages.

Because the Walt Disney creations have made such an impact worldwide, in 1970 the Disney family and the management of Walt Disney Productions decided to create an archive where the history of Walt Disney and the entire Disney organization could be collected, preserved, and made available to qualified researchers.

The Walt Disney Archives began operations on June 22, 1970, when I was hired to be the archivist. I had been a reference librarian in the University Research Library at UCLA for the previous five years, and while there I had prepared an extensive Disney bibliography. In order to provide space for the Archives, the Disney Studio opened up the wing of the Animation Building containing Walt Disney's office. It had been closed since his death. We set up our office in one of the anterooms, and used others for storage.

As we collected materials, our needs for storage space continued to grow. We took over closets, attics, basements, and corners wherever we could. Within a few years, we were given a 1,000-square-foot storage area, but it was in a building three miles away, and on a mezzanine accessible only by forklift or narrow stairway. The offices of the Archives were later moved into two of our former small storerooms. In 1976, a large office building was constructed at the Studio, and an audio-visual area on the first floor, and a large storage area on the basement floor. The storeroom features temperature and humidity controls.

The collections of the Archives cover the entire range of the Disney enterprises. Basic, of course, are the files, awards, office furnishings,

David R. Smith is Archivist for the Walt Disney Archives in Burbank, California.

and personal memorabilia of Walt Disney himself. There are also correspondence files and memorabilia of Walt Disney's brother Roy, and a collection has been made on the genealogy of the Disney family. Material telling the history of the Disney motion pictures, animated and live action, takes many forms. For the animated films, there are story-meeting notes, story sketches, drafts (which list sequence and animator), orginal artwork, cels, backgrounds, and cutting continuities. Some notable props and costumes have been saved from live action films, in addition to scripts and various production files. Walking through the Archives storeroom you might notice a Borgia portrait painted for *The Shaggy Dog* next to a miniature dirigible used for *Island at the Top of the World*. There is Annette Funicello's Mouseketeer outfit, Mary Poppins' carousel horse, and a *20,000 Leagues Under the Sea* diving helmet.

Publicity files provide backup to the production records. There are press releases, press books, posters, lobby cards, and campaign kits. Disney has had a clipping service since 1924, and the result has been a gigantic collection of press clippings. Besides reviews of the films, there are newspaper and magazine articles about Walt Disney, the Studio, Disneyland, and Walt Disney World. Major magazine articles have been catalogued as if they were books, with author and subject entries.

The Archives has a relatively complete collection of domestic Disney books (over 800 titles) and comic books. It also boasts a very large collection of foreign books and comics, some of them simply translations of the American publications, but others written and illustrated in the foreign countries. There are also sets of Disney phonograph records, sheet music, and song folios. Besides having tens of thousands of still photographs, including 8,000 pictures of Walt Disney, the Archives has access to over half a million still negatives.

One area which sets the Disney Archives apart from many other business archives is its collection of Disney character merchandise. This collection consists of toys, games, and clothing made not by Disney but under license by various manufacturers. The Disney characters have been used on everything imaginable, from drinking glasses to puppets, from sleds to linoleum. The early Disneyana, as it is called, has become especially popular with collectors in recent years, and prices of the watches, figurines, dolls, and toys have sky-rocketed.

The Archives is not only interested in the past. It is actively preserving the records of the present which will be useful to future historians. Thus, periodic shipments are received of all items printed in the company's two print shops (at the Studio and Walt Disney World). Disneyland and Walt Disney World send examples of guide books, souvenir merchandise, advertising, menus, ticket media, employee publications, surveys, as well as correspondence files of key administrators.

Films are not stored physically in the Archives because of their needs for special film vaults, but accurate records are kept of them. The Archives has been instrumental in finding almost forty previously lost Disney films from the silent era which have been added to the company's collection.

Because of the current interest in film history and the impact of motion pictures on American culture, it is lamentable that more movie studios have not taken steps to preserve and catalog their archives and make them available for research. The Disney Archives has made great strides in the past nine years, and is doing its part in preserving Hollywood's past. Perhaps other studios can be persuaded to follow its lead.

PLAYER PIANO ROLLS IN THE COLLECTION OF THE SONGWRITERS' HALL OF FAME

by Ginnine Cocuzza

Player piano rolls are a complex element of popular American musical history. A single roll at once represents a piece of music and often its lyrics, the performer and his playing style, the recording industry at its roots, and the establishment of popular home musical entertainment.

To the twentieth-century American, a home without a radio or record player is inconceivable. Yet only 100 years ago, a brief span of time by today's reckoning, to have music in the home a family had to have a musically-inclined member and the instrument on which to play. The piano was probably the most popular and accessible home instrument but it was not often played with great skill. While Thomas Edison was attempting to preserve the human voice on tinfoil cylinders, piano manufacturers in Europe and America were already perfecting a mechanism which could reproduce the performance of a concert pianist in a home or public place.

Patent rights for the use of pneumatic mechanisms in a piano were issued in the United States as early as 1860. The original pianola was a portable mechanism placed in front of the piano keyboard. It had a 65-note span and actually struck the keys to play the piano. The first "push-up" piano player to achieve commercial success was the Pianista in France in 1863. The pianola was invented by the American engineer E. S. Votey, for which he was granted a patent in 1897. Pianola was originally the patent trade name for the instrument reproduced by the Aeolian Company of England and the United States, but the name quickly passed into public domain to imply the home player piano. By 1910, the player piano with the mechanism inside appeared, and by 1915 the "push-up" variety ceased to be manufactured. The playing action was least conspicuously installed in the upright piano, but with the advent of the more sophisticated repro-

Ginnine Cocuzza is a doctoral candidate in the Graduate Drama Department of New York University.

ducer mechanisms, installations in beautifully styled grand pianos were profitably achieved.

Between 1900 and 1930 approximately 2½ million player pianos were installed in American homes, not counting all those in places of entertainment. By 1950, most had been dismantled or completely destroyed. Today they are collectors' items, a living moment of American musical history. The player piano and other automatic musical instruments all used paper music rolls. Companies like Welte Mignon Deluxe, Aeolian Duo Art, Ampico, and Recordo made rolls only for their own specialized mechanisms. Others made rolls for the coin-operated instruments. By 1902, the 88-note roll had been adopted as standard for commercial and home player pianos. Since most non-reproducing mechanisms were purchased from the Standard Pneumatic Action Company or the Auto Pneumatic Action Company and installed by the piano manufacturers in their own instruments, the standard 88-note roll could be manufactured and sold by anyone with the right equipment. And they did, most of them companies of which only their box labels remain to prove their existence. Most expression rolls could also be played on a standard player piano.

The master for a piano roll could be created in one of two ways. For the first and earliest method, the roll never came near a piano until it was ready to be tested. Alexander Buchner, historian of the player piano, described the technique:

> The "metronome" method produced music in which every bar was of the same duration, as if timed by metronome. This was produced by means of a prepared scheme showing the distance between holes on the perforated sheet and the same distance for note-lengths. Each note of the piece of music to be recorded was marked on the appropriate place in the scheme; duration was shown by a stroke at the point where the perforation was to be made. When the whole piece had been marked in this way a machine perforated the strip, which was then tested on the pianola; any mistakes could then be corrected. This produced a master-roll from which cardboard matrices could be made; rolls could then be perforated in numbers.

This method lacked any of the subtle fluctuations in tempo inevitable when the same piece of music is played by hand. More patent applications were filed and a second method on which all subsequent expression and reproducing methods are based was devised. Again, Buchner's description:

The perforated strips were produced by means of a Morse code recording made during the musician's performance. As he played the piano every key, when touched, set electric current in motion; the electromagnets then affected the recording mechanism according to the force of each note struck. Small errors in the pianist's performance could be corrected on the test roll which was usually supervised and approved by the artist.

Early "push-up" piano player rolls had only a 44-note span. For popular home use, the 65-note roll was most common until the mechanism was placed inside the piano and full 88-note span was achieved. For a few years, player pianos were built with tracker bars designed to accommodate both 65- and 88-note rolls. The majority of rolls in any collection will be of the standard 88-note variety.

Each roll originally came in its own box. The box label on the end identifies the company label, the song title, the song's catalogue number, and any combination of the following: composer(s), copyrights, performer(s), arranger, price, and music category (fox trot, waltz, rag, etc.). The roll leader usually has the same label printed or pasted on it plus tempo and expression settings. Some rolls have red or green expression lines which must be followed manually by the human piano player. Most song rolls have the lyrics printed on the righthand margin for singing along.

Some roll leaders are more interesting than others. The Q-R-S Autograph Word Roll series, which dates back to 1916 or earlier, features the signature of the performing artist on the leader. The Rythmodik Song Roll leaders have large released rolls and descriptions of the Broadway revue "your new Irving Berlin hit is from." The recent Q-R-S Celebrity Series rolls have a large label with the photo, autograph, and biography of the performer. Occasionally special rolls were printed for the distributor's window display, the message either rolling by while the piano played or draped gracefully across the keys, bench, and floor. Reproducer rolls often had beautifully printed leaders but these were usually classical rolls.

Piano roll boxes are generally uninteresting except for the label. A rarity is Perfection 86708 "Oh Joe With Your Fiddle and Bow" which has an advertisement for Bloomingdale's on the lid.

When it was time to select music, European player piano manufacturers reached first for the classics. Welte and Sons, with the perfection of hand-played and then the reproducing rolls, recorded many of the finest pianists in Europe. Stravinsky arranged and recorded the *Fire Bird Suite* for the Aeolian Company on six continuous rolls. But Americans had other music they wanted to hear: popular music for singing and dancing. Composers of operettas and musical revues were at the top of their lists: Rudolf Friml, Irving Berlin, Victor Herbert, George Gershwin. Often the composer was also the artist playing the roll: George Gershwin, Eubie Blake, "Fats" Waller. Specialty piano duos like Phil Ohman and Victor Arden, so popular they were considered essential to the success of the new Adele and Fred Astaire musical in 1924, also cut music rolls. Piano rolls made available songs and styles of music which might not have been heard outside of New York City. Ragtime, in particular, was popularized by the piano; early phonograph records could not reproduce the quality of the piano well until the 1920s. Around 1906, Scott Joplin made piano rolls which reproduce his actual piano playing without editing. These were 65-note rolls some of which have been converted to 88-note and are available through Q-R-S. Ragtime faded away with the player piano, overwhelmed by the phonograph, talking pictures, and radio.

The 88-note piano roll is a twenty-foot length of paper attached to a cardboard core with plastic or metal flanges at either end and housed in a cardboard box. All rules for paper storage and conservation apply plus special consideration for the characteristics of the roll and box. Cool humidity-controlled shelf storage is recommended with rolls stacked no more than four high on each shelf; shelves should be exactly one box-length deep. Most damage to the Hall of Fame collection has been to the boxes, especially the corners, bottoms, and lids. Unless the box itself is extraordinary, these can be inexpensively replaced through Q-R-S. Conservation materials manufacturers will custom fabricate acid-free boxes of the exact size needed.

If the rolls are handled properly, the paper does not come into contact with the box sides and a properly handled box will last a long time. The label from the old box may be removed and attached to the new one. If the label is unsalvable or missing, *all* the information from the old label or the leader imprint should be typed on a new pressure-sensitive label and attached to the new box.

Piano roll paper is reputed to be hightly acidic. However, except for slight yellowing and occasional leader damage where it is most touched by hand, the collection at the Songwriters' Hall of Fame is generally speaking in good condition. A few leader tabs and end flanges need to be replaced and all the very old rolls should be checked for edge damage before any attempt is made to play them. The rolls should not be unrolled more than a few feet of a roll without the proper equipment to avoid damaging them. With patience most damaged rolls can be repaired. While there are differences of opinion among the following articles, all give excellent detailed instructions for common repairs to piano rolls:

Q. David Bowers, "Care and Repair of Music Rolls," *Encyclo-pedia of Automatic Musical Instruments,* p. 75

Palmer Mai, "Roll Maintenance and Repair Tips," *Perforated Paper Patter,* pp.30-40.

Arthur Sanders, "Care and Repair of Paper Music Rolls," in *Silver Anniversary Collection of the Musical Box Society International,* pp.783-84.

When the older (1930 and before) piano rolls were new and unused, each had a paper seal wrapped around the roll. These rolls should probably remain unused while a duplicate is available in other collections.

For the piano roll collection to be accessible for research, it must be catalogued. However, the manner in which the piano rolls are catalogued necessarily affects the cataloguing of the entire collection of the Songwriters' Hall of Fame. Logical correlations among the various objects become evident in an integrated catalogue. A researcher looking up George Gershwin will find books, records, and sheet music in the section of the card catalogue under his name. The form an integrated catalogue will take should be decided by a professional cataloguer and the staff who have to maintain it.

The cataloguing of sheet music at the Songwriters' Hall of Fame on 3 x 5" carbon-set forms provides the model for music rolls:

Title: After the Ball (Music Roll)
Composer: Charles K. Harris
Perf. by:
Label: U.S. Player Music Rolls 40963
Mfr: United States Music Co.
Copyright: 1892, Charles K. Harris
        88-note standard, Waltz, tempo 80
Gift of: Bill Simon

When a piano roll enters the Collection, it is registered and accessioned. Both the object and its container are of interest to the Collection and should be so designated by the accession number plus a lower case (a) for the box and (b) for the roll. If the box has been discarded and replaced or if the roll enters the Collection without a box, this should be noted on the accession form: "not in original box." For cataloguing purposes, the roll and box are considered as a unit.

A piano roll, like phonograph discs and tapes, is not only an audiorecord, it is also a piece of music. Complete information pertaining to both must be included on the catalogue card. If any of the particulars are missing, research effort must be made to fill in the information. These fill-ins are usually indicated in brackets. If the information cannot be found, the card should indicate "imprint obscured" or "imprint missing."

Audiorecords and music catalogue cards usually show duration in minutes; for the piano roll, the note length and tempo markings are cited as well as the particular instrument on which the roll should be played. (*Example:* 88-note standard, tempo 70; *or* 88-note Duo Art reproducer, tempo 65.)

As the Collection is dependent upon donors for many of its acquisitions, the source of the gift is shown on the catalogue card and the accession form. If the source is unknown, "F.I.C.," Found in Collection is indicated.

The cards should be kept in a separate piano roll file. If they are interfiled with the sheet music, the media designation (piano roll), should be added after or under the title. If separate files are kept, additional information cards should be made for the title and its added entries for a complete cross-reference:

```
Herbert, Victor.

   Additional information on this subject will be found in the
catalogues listed below:

__ Piano Rolls
__ Sheet Music
__ Clipping Files
__ Library
```

The main entry system recommended by the American Library
Association assumes that classification will be determined by author
or composer. Therefore the initial or main entry card is here filed by
composer with tracings for the added entries; possible subject headings are also shown:

```
Herbert, Victor.

   Ah! Sweet Mystery of Life. (Audiorecord)
Lyrics by Rida Johnson Young. Pianostyle Music Co. 30536.
[1910]
   1 piano roll. 88-note. tempo 60-85.
   B. G. Howard, pianist.
   From Naughty Marietta, operetta.
   F.I.C.

1. Music, popular. 2. Music, operetta.
I. Young, Rida Johnson. II. Howard, B. G.
III. Title.
```

Since the media designation (Audiorecord) does not tell us whether
this is a disc or tape much less piano roll, the qualifier, "piano roll,"
and number of pieces contained, "1," must be shown. For this and
the following card forms, it is assumed that the roll is made for all
standard player pianos and exceptions only are noted with the qualifier. A full set of cards for the tracings:

Young, Rida Johnson.

Ah! Sweet Mystery of Life. (Audiorecord)
Music by Victor Herbert. Pianostyle Music Co. 30536.
[1910]
   1 piano roll. 88-note. tempo 60-85.
   B. G. Howard, pianist.
   From *Naughty Marietta,* operetta.
   F.I.C.

   1. Music, popular. 2. Music, operetta.
   I. Herbert, Victor. II. Howard, B. G. III. Title.

Howard, B. G.

Ah! Sweet Mystery of Life. (Audiorecord)
Music by Victor Herbert. Lyrics by Rida Johnson Young.
Pianostyle Music Co. 30536. [1910]
   1 piano roll. 88-note. tempo 60-85.
   From *Naughty Marietta,* operetta.
   F.I.C.

   1. Music, popular. 2. Music, operetta.
   I. Herbert, Victor. II. Young, Rida Johnson.
   III. Title.

Ah! Sweet Mystery of Life.

   (Audiorecord) Music by Victor Herbert.
Lyrics by Rida Johnson Young. Pianostyle Music Co. 30536.
[1910]
   1 piano roll. 88-note. tempo 60-85.
   B. G. Howard, pianist.
   From *Naughty Marietta,* operetta.
   F.I.C.

   1. Music, popular. 2. Music, operetta.
   I. Herbert, Victor. II. Young, Rida Johnson.
   III. Howard, B. G.

Added entries (i.e., to show arranger or extended contents) can be described in separate lines.

The most familiar unit entry system is the Catalogue of the Library of Congress. All the information and tracings are organized on one card. Duplicate cards totaling all the tracings plus one constitute a set. The purchasing library enters the appropriate heading on each card and the job is done. The Library of Congress has begun including phonograph discs in their catalogue but, unfortunately, not piano rolls. However, the LC form can be used to set up a unit system with additional descriptive information added to the unit sets.

Until recently, American audiorecord and music collections accessible to the public have not interested themselves in piano rolls because of the special care they need. Fortunately, this attitude is not universal as exemplified by the fact that the major Ampico collection including five reproducing grand pianos and 2,000 of the 4,500 rolls manufactured by the company will eventually be housed in the British Institute of Recorded Sound. The piano roll collection at the Songwriters' Hall of Fame will continue to grow because of the special nature of its archives. They are making a serious attempt to accumulate and preserve these audiorecords not merely because of their musical content but because they represent a special and historical medium by which recorded music is conveyed to the public.

THE SAN FRANCISCO ARCHIVES
FOR THE PERFORMING ARTS

by R. Eric Gustafson

In the Presidio section of San Francisco near the Pacific Heights sits the usual modern institutional adaptation of a neoclassical building. It is surrounded by a well-tended lawn with attractive trees. Obviously, this is the local public library. The major difference between the numerous public libraries that dot the many cities and towns across the nation and the Presidio branch library is that this one houses in its basement a treasure trove unique in all America.

The curious or interested visitor may notice upon entering through the back staircase a tall, slim, blond man either in midst of setting up a new exhibition or lugging in a carton of newly acquired material for the permanent collection. This collection represents the unstinting energy of Russell Hartley, who for more than thirty-five years has been collecting and preserving the ephemeral droppings of the performing arts in the San Francisco area.

Russell Hartley was for many years a dancer and costume designer for the ballet when he was not filling his home with performing arts memorabilia in this historically important area in California. Finally in 1975, he opened the San Francisco Archives for the Performing Arts as its founding director.

The Archives is an autonomous, nonprofit organization with a board of directors and a dues-paying membership of just over three hundred. It is set up as a museum, library, and research facility open free to the public. It represents the first serious attempt by any individual or organization to fully chronicle the day-to-day theatrical history of the San Francisco Bay Area from the Gold Rush to the present.

Mr. Hartley is helped in this mammoth undertaking by Judith Solomon, his assistant director, who is an expert in library services and copes with the daily running of the Archives.

R. Eric Gustafson is a theatre design consultant.

As a museum, the Archives researches, designs, and installs exhibitions at the War Memorial Opera House for the San Francisco Opera, the San Francisco Ballet, and the San Francisco Symphony. Other exhibitions have been installed at the main branch of the San Francisco Public Library for Black History Month, Agnes de Mille, and the Joffrey Ballet Company, to name a few. Maintained at the Archives at 3150 Sacramento Street is an exhibition area with displays which change at three-month intervals.

As a library and research facility, the Archives keeps up-to-date files on individual performers in all fields of the performing arts, their companies, the productions they made famous, and the theatres they performed in. These files contain programs, photographs, flyers, reviews, articles and all manner of materials which help tell any given history. The Archives maintains over 180 volumes of daily clippings from the amusement sections of local newspapers. The accumulation of magazines and periodicals from the 1850s to the present contains invaluable descriptions of performances and daily theatre activity.

Among the rare and unusual items in the Archives collection is an original drawing of Vittorio Arimondi by Enrico Caruso (1920) ; an original score penned by Arturo Toscanini and autographed by him in 1903; a painting of Marie Taglioni (as "La Gitana"), the greatest ballerina of the Romantic period, by Joseph Rubens Powell; and photographs of Raymond and Isadora Duncan, whose father opened a bank in San Francisco in 1874. Of particular interest is the extremely rare photograph of Isadora Duncan at age twelve taken in Fresno in 1889. Until the Archives discovered it, this original photograph had never been published. The Archives has more than fifty costumes including Goncharova's from *Le Coq d'Or* and one worn by Alexandra Danilova in her most famous role in *Beau Danube*. Material salvaged from the earthquake and fire of 1906, although largely in reproduced form, represents all that survived.

Transcriptions of interviews with contemporary artists and historical figures like Sarah Bernhardt; old and rare phonograph records together with new records (some re-renderings of old classics) ; figurines, fans, stage accessories, and mementos from historic San Francisco theatres round out this unique collection.

The San Francisco Archives for the Performing Arts is located beneath the Presidio Branch of the San Francisco Library (although operated independently of the San Francisco Library) at 3150 Sacramento Street, San Francisco, California 94115. (Telephone: 415-922-6750)

INVENTORY

Bound volumes, all theatrical: estimated 2,000

Unbound periodicals: 8,000

Bound periodicals: 94 volumes

Periodicals, theatre sections, dance news, etc.: 3,600

Loose leaf binders, with historical day-to-day information (average of 300 pages each, many pages having information on both sides): 257 volumes

Acid-free storage boxes with particularized collections (sheet music, photographs, scrapbooks, etc.): 117

Large storage boxes mainly with file collections on specific subjects (San Francisco Symphony, San Francisco Opera, San Francisco Ballet, Metropolitan Ballet, Ballet Russe de Monte Carlo, Ballet Theatre, Diaghileff Ballet, De Basil Ballet Russe, Joffrey Ballet): 55

Alphabetical file primarily on individuals and theatrical organizations: 60 drawers

Additional file boxes with particular collections (Isadora Duncan, Martha Graham, San Francisco historical photographs, movie stills, etc.): 50

Slides made from visuals in archives collections: 2,872

Special albums containing such ephemera as circus memorabilia and trade cards: 20

Negatives (historical): 800

Negatives (San Francisco Ballet): 3,000

Negatives (miscellaneous): 1,000

Sheet music contained in boxes already accounted for (estimate):
10,000 covers

Posters: 2,000

Framed materials (mostly old and rare): 800 pieces

Records (78 rpm recordings of Caruso, Galli Curci, early black music,
variety artists, Bert Williams, Paul Whiteman, minstrel, vaudeville,
etc.): 2,500

Records (33⅓ rpm recordings of artists of lasting interest and re-
recordings of classics): 1,000

Tapes (interviews of contemporary artists and tapes of historical
figures like Sarah Bernhardt): 100

Photographs (contained in files and boxes already accounted for):
18,000 to 25,000

Photographs of San Francisco Ballet: 10,000

Photographs of movies and related: 10,000

Scrapbooks (containing rare programs, photos, clippings, etc. mostly
relating to San Francisco): 100

Theatrical prints (including engravings, etchings, woodcuts, chro-
mos, lithographs, etc.): 12,000

Picture material (such as found in periodicals, of theatrical personalities, events, etc.; these are often all that remains of those artists
working before the 1906 fire and earthquake): 50,000

Artifacts (figurines, theatrical plates, fans, castenets, combs, stage
accessories from historic San Francisco theatres): 500

Costumes (Goncharova, *Le Coq d'Or,* San Francisco Ballet's *Jinx,*
Danilova, *Beau Danube,* Vollmar, *Swan,* etc.): 50

Costume plates (most from San Francisco Ballet): 200

Cartons of unfiled materials of all kinds: 50

INDEX